Ask yourself —

What kind of person am I if I do not help make this world better?

Don't leave this book behind. Get it. Read it. Live it. Breathe it. Share it. And Go! Change *your* World! And change *the* World!

Acknowledgements

This book would have never come to fruition had it not been for the encouragement and support of Daniel Erickson. Thank you for reading and re-reading each and every draft and painstakingly giving me your feedback. You truly make this world a better place.

Thank you also to (in alphabetic order) Clare Austen, Rita Connor, Debbie Cristefar, Patricia Keel, Richard Snowden and Ellen Wagner for your loving and generous suggestions. My world is richer because you are all in it.

Thank you from my heart to my mother and father and sister. You have always believed in me. Every moment with you has been a cherished moment. You have always understood me inside out. You have always encouraged me to bring out my hidden strengths. You are proof that we can all change this world.

Last but not least, thank you to all my readers and audiences across the world. Thank you for being you. I cherish all of you.

Yes, You Can Change the World

Aman Motwane

Prakash Press

Prakash Press
P.O. Box 4268
Redondo Beach, CA 90277

Library of Congress Cataloging-in-Publication Data

Motwane, Aman,
Yes, You Can Change The World,
p. cm.
ISBN-10 0-9671350-5-2 hardcover
ISBN-13 978-0-9671350-5-2 hardcover

1. Success in business.   2. Interpersonal relations.   3. Self-management.
4. Peace of mind.   5. Conduct of life.   I. Title.

Yes,
You Can
Change the
World

A Parable

An Ending

He had expected barely a dozen. Instead, there were hundreds. So many people, too many to count.

A huddled mass of people moving in slow unison. Waiting to pay their last respects to the man he knew as his father.

He had expected so few.

The sky was the color of tar. Rain came down in sheets. A few people were hunched under umbrellas. The rest struggled forward, heads bent against the relentless rain, mud riding on their shoes.

He had never seen so many crowding this town.

He had never seen so many out-of-state license plates.

Why had they braved this weather? he wondered. *Why had they travelled from so far?*

Squeezing his eyes shut as if to keep out the pain, he asked himself the most important question, *How had Father touched so many?*

As he looked through the rain hammering on the windshield, memories of the last time he had been with his father came rushing back.

Had it been a year ago?

He had become so consumed by ambition, his visits had become less and less frequent.

Now, he remembered standing at his father's doorstep, exchanging goodbyes, just before heading back to the big city where his practice devoured his time.

He could still feel his father's embrace.

And just as he had countless times before, his father had leaned over and whispered into his ear, "Make a difference in the world!"

The young man scanned the crowd before him. *What exactly did Father do to make a difference? How did he make a difference for so many?*

Wiping his tears on his sleeve, he thought, *If I died tomorrow, would anyone notice? How many would come to my funeral?*

Again, his father's image flickered before him. He recalled a conversation they'd had just a couple of years before. He could still see his father's face, his eyes radiating kindness and patience.

"To make a difference in the world, you must go beyond merely *doing* things," his father had said.

"Whenever you *do* things for others, you make a difference but only *for a short time*. You feed them, and soon they are hungry again. You clothe them, and soon they are cold and bare again. And you can never give them enough money, no matter how much you give.

"But there is a way to change the world that is far easier, far more lasting, and far more powerful!"

He could still hear his father's hoarse whisper, "Most people focus on *doing* things as the way to make a difference. What they don't realize is that the most powerful way to make a difference doesn't require you to actually *do* anything at all!"

What exactly had Father been talking about? he now wondered.

The young man had been groomed in the world of business, where action and execution are *everything*. Nothing happens until you get off your seat and actually *do* something.

His father's claim that you can make a difference without doing anything was so alien to his nature, he had completely dismissed it.

Now he wished he had paid closer attention.

He dropped his head in resignation. *So this is the way it is. This is how it all finally ends.*

He had never imagined things would end this way —

incomplete, unresolved, with so much left unspoken and unshared.

How could you leave me like this?

He pushed his arm against his mouth in a futile attempt to muffle his sobs.

Now how will I ever learn your secrets?

In that moment, he remembered something his father used to say. "Some things end so that other things can begin."

The sky crackled with lightning. The roar of thunder overwhelmed his senses. He turned on his windshield wipers and, as they pushed the rain aside, he saw again the long line of people snaking their way through the wet grass.

He realized his father's secret wasn't lost at all. It was right here in front of him!

Surely one of these people knows the secret. Maybe they all know!

Maybe this ending leads to a new beginning!

A chill ran up his spine. He resolved to learn the secret before the day was over.

Resolutely, he got out of his car, hunched against the rain and ran to join the line of people inching forward.

A New Perspective

As the young man raced forward, a deep pain inside compelled him to stop. Doubt had begun to creep in.

Over the years, he had distanced himself from those who weren't as successful as him. He had shunned the efforts of his cousins and classmates to contact him.

Does anyone here remember me? Is anyone expecting me?

Perhaps if he had stayed in touch, he would have known earlier that his father was in the hospital with just a few days left. Perhaps he would have known to expect such a large crowd.

As he joined the line, he thought to himself, *Perhaps it will be easy for me to mingle in and learn my father's secret. Perhaps I'll finally learn what I need to learn.*

He had barely been in line a few moments when a hoarse voice whispered over his shoulder, "Your father was a great man."

He turned and saw a woman, about his age and height.

Rain was running in rivulets down her face. Her expensively-cut designer suit was soaked.

He wondered how this complete stranger could possibly know who he was.

"You're his son, aren't you? I can see the resemblance!" she exclaimed as though she'd read his mind.

Brushing strands of wet hair from her eyes, she added, "He talked so often, so lovingly, about you."

Placing her hand on his shoulder, she said, "You must be crushed. He was such a wonderful human being. He changed my life completely. He changed my whole world!"

He stood there for a moment, his hands trembling, uncertain of what to say or do next. In a gush of emotion, he turned to her and asked, "How did you know my father? What did he do to change your life?"

She frowned as though she didn't quite understand. Then she tilted her head upwards and gazed pensively into the distance.

"He believed in me!" she said finally, her voice quivering.

"He believed in you?" He raised his eyebrows.

She nodded, looking deeply into his eyes. "He believed in me when no one else did. He believed in me when I didn't believe in myself."

The young man looked puzzled. "But what did he *do* for

you?" he asked. He tried to banish the thoughts coursing through his mind. *Did Father give her a job? Did he help her pay her way through school? Did he loan her money?*

The woman smiled. "He didn't actually *do* anything for me at all!"

He felt his breath slowly leak out of him.

How can you make a difference in someone's life without doing anything for them? he wondered again.

She stepped back and examined him up and down. "I've known your father for about a year, but I don't think I've seen you here before."

Something cracked inside the young man in that moment, as if a dam filled with years of guilt and anger had burst open. "I was too absorbed in myself, too caught up in my own life. You haven't seen me before because I hardly came here."

He sobbed quietly, lips clenched together, tears drenching his face again. "But now I'm finally here. And I want. I need. I desperately need. To know my father. Please. Help me. I've lost so much time."

She squeezed his hand, nodding that she understood. "I know all about what you're going through. I, too, have a history of staying away from those who love me."

The young man studied the rain and tears on the woman's face, noticing how one was indistinguishable from another.

She said, "Probably the best way to understand your father is to understand the effect he had on others."

He looked up, alert and eager for her to continue.

She smiled. "We all respected him so much, we never called him by his name. We called him Father. Just … Father. I think he liked that."

She swallowed as if debating whether to continue. "My life was a mess when I first met him."

Hastily, she pulled a tissue out of her purse and dabbed her eyes. "Everyone used to tell me I had everything, that I was the one most likely to succeed. I had the looks. The talent. The smarts. I was a hard worker. But inside, I felt hollow. Empty. I kept wondering about the point of it all. It all seemed so unnecessary."

She stared at the drenched tissue paper in her hand, seemed to recognize the futility of using it in the rain, and slumped her shoulder with frustration. "After years and years of working, I felt as though I had accomplished nothing.

"I tried changing jobs. Changing friends. Changing cities. I left everything behind and came here, far away from everyone and everything. But the emptiness, the hollowness wouldn't go away.

"I tried books, workshops, all kinds of programs, support groups, therapists. But nothing changed."

They both looked at the tissue in her hand. She had

worked it into a small ball. "I tried to find comfort in food. Drugs. Sex. But it didn't matter what I tried, what I changed, the emptiness just didn't go away.

"I had hit rock bottom when I met your father. I felt lost. Hopeless. Burned out."

The young man felt his jaw tighten. The moment had finally arrived, he realized. The moment when she would reveal how his father had changed her whole world.

She closed her eyes and spread her arms out, palms facing upwards. He saw the rain gathering in her palms. In barely a whisper, she continued. "Things started looking up after I met your father!

"It was the most unusual thing. Somehow, I always felt so special whenever I was with him.

"His face would light up when he saw me. Just like that. It's as though he saw things in me I didn't see in myself. I had a tremendous sense that he just believed in me.

"He never compared me to others. Never let me feel I wasn't good enough. Never told me to cheer up. Never gave me that tired, old line about how things will all turn out for the better. He just believed in me!

"For the first time in my life, I started feeling good about being me — *just* me! For the first time, I started feeling happy. I started feeling a calmness I didn't know was possible."

She curled her hands toward herself and looked at her

fingertips. He noticed a diamond ring on her left hand. She followed his gaze and added, "All this — all this success — happened after I met your father! If he hadn't discovered me, I might have never discovered myself!"

The young man started to ask a question but stopped when he realized she wasn't quite done.

She continued, "A few weeks ago …" Abruptly, she stopped. Her lips quivered for a brief moment, then she covered her face in her hands.

He moved closer to her and put his hand on her shoulder. Slowly, her trembling subsided. Gazing into his eyes, she exclaimed, "It was just a few weeks ago!"

She dabbed her eyes with the back of her hands. "A few weeks ago, over a cup of tea, I asked your father why he believed in me so much …"

I am the Young Woman

It was one of those lazy afternoons. Father and I were sitting on his porch. I was breathless with excitement. I told him about my recent promotion. My recent engagement. I showed him my new ring.

As I looked at him, his shrivelled head slightly bent, his parched lips slightly puckered over his teacup, his sunken eyes partly closed, I marvelled once again at how much my life had changed since I'd met him.

Father cradled my face in his hands and exclaimed, "I knew it! I knew it! I knew you were destined for great things!"

As he held my face, I realized I had never felt more alive. I felt as though the world could throw any challenge at me and I would still triumph.

In that joyous moment, a question that had been lurking in the back of my mind for quite some time came bubbling up to the surface.

I cupped my hands around his and asked teary-eyed,

"Father, why do you believe in me so much? You believed in me right from the beginning, when I was a total, complete stranger to you, when you didn't know anything about me!"

Father tilted his head slightly as if to say, "Isn't it obvious?"

I shook my head. "No, it's not obvious. Not to me. Tell me! Why do you have such a deep faith in me? Why do you have such a deep faith in all the people in your life?"

The answer he gave me changed my perspective completely! It changed how I experience everyone and everything in this world! It changed me! I don't think I'll see the world in the same way ever again!

Placing his palm on his chest, Father took a deep breath. "Most people already know what I'm about to tell you, but few really believe it!"

"Believe what?"

He tapped his heart with his hand. "Few believe it in here."

"In their hearts?"

He nodded. "Very few believe in their heart that every man and every woman has an intrinsic worth in this world. Very few believe that every man and every woman, no matter what they do or what their background, has a special purpose in this world."

The answer he had given me sounded so simple, so obvious. But I knew Father was a man of many layers and that we had barely scratched the surface, so I asked him, "But don't they teach us that in all the books and in all the scriptures?"

"Yes, we all say it and we all write about it because it sounds good and it feels good. But so few believe it. Even fewer understand it. And hardly anyone practices it."

He leaned back and stated, "Knowledge without practice is the same as *no* knowledge."

He paused to let that sink in.

Then he continued, "If we all believed it and if we all practiced it, the whole world would be a different place."

Just then, I noticed a scraggly-looking person pushing a shopping cart across the street. I could hear the click-click of metal against metal as the the cart wobbled forward.

Nodding toward the homeless person, I said, "Sometimes it's difficult to see the special purpose of some individuals."

Father followed my gaze. "Just because you can't see it, doesn't mean it isn't there."

We both sat there quietly, looking across the street, until the shopping cart disappeared around the corner.

Father tilted his face toward the corner. "When most people look at a person like that, they look right through them. As though they're completely inconsequential, as though they aren't even there."

He leaned back in his chair. "You know what I see? I see a unique individual with a significant, special purpose in this universe. With an intrinsic worth and value. For the world and for me."

I frowned, trying to see what he saw.

He looked at me and smiled. "The intrinsic worth is often not immediately apparent. Maybe that person has a special insight. Maybe that person can do something in a way that others can't. Maybe there's a special time when that person will come into your life and change everything. It doesn't matter. All you have to *know* is that the worth is in there, that this is the way of the world."

He tapped his chest again. "It all starts from deep within you. A recognition. An awareness. A belief. A way of looking at everyone and everything. A way of living. A way of life.

"If you believe the worth is in there, you will see it.

"You will see it in a homeless person. You will see it in a difficult person. You will even see it in someone who is not very likeable at first.

"If you believe it, you'll see it.

"Remember that old saying — seeing is believing? I've found that, more often than not, you must believe it *before* you will see it."

I studied his face for a moment. "You make it sound like this is the most important thing in the world."

He gazed at me. "It is. And here's why. You may not realize it, but in every interaction, in every exchange, in every transaction with another human being, you either cut them down or you build them up.

"If you don't believe in others' worth, whether you realize it or not, you are cutting them down. That's because they can sense that you don't believe in them. They can see it in your eyes, in your face, in everything you do and everything you say to them.

"On the other hand, when you believe in their worth, you can't help but build them up. That's because they can see that in your eyes as well. They can see it in the way you look at them, in the way you smile at them, in everything you do and everything you say to them.

"How you see, what you believe — *who you are!* — communicates a lot more than anything you actually do or say."

Tapping his chest again for emphasis, he added, "Something magical happens when you believe in the intrinsic worth of a human being! It's contagious! When you believe, it's a matter of time before the other person believes it too. It's a matter of time before the other person builds up courage and self esteem. And all that leads to beautiful things — like this joyous news you've brought me today!"

I felt tears building up. His belief in me had changed my whole world!

I squeezed his bony fingers with gratitude.

He smiled back. "When you believe in another person, it's as though you bring light into their world. And this light not only illuminates their world, it also illuminates everyone around them."

I frowned. "What if you're not quite sure of a particular person? Can you believe *somewhat* in their worth? Is that enough?"

Father snorted, "Either you believe or you don't. If you're trying to believe or if you're not quite sure, it's the same as not believing."

He leaned back. "Make no mistake. Either you build them up. Or, you cut them down. There's no middle ground."

I asked, "So you assume that all strangers are special in some way? Is that what happened when you first met me? You didn't exactly know what made me special, but you acted as though I must have been special?"

Father shook his head vigorously. "I didn't assume. I didn't act. I didn't pretend. I didn't force myself. I just *knew* you were. I just *believed*. The difference might be small. But this small difference makes all the difference in the world! Acting or assuming or pretending requires effort. Believing, on the other hand, is effortless."

He cleared his throat. "Believing is free. It doesn't cost you anything. You don't have to do anything. And yet, you can change the world for everyone around you!"

He remained quiet for a while. After a moment of sitting silently by his side, I realized he was breathing hard. He pulled a tissue out of a box and dabbed the corner of his mouth.

When his hard breathing seemed to subside, he called my name. I looked up.

"I know deep down you already know that everyone has a special purpose in this life," he told me.

I nodded silently.

"Now you have to go from knowing to believing!"

"How? It sounds a bit difficult!"

He put his hand over his chest and shook his head miserably. His breathing had become labored again. He clutched his chest to calm himself. In spurts, he responded, "You just have to. Make three simple shifts. In your perspective."

Alarm shot up my spine as I noticed a change in his posture. His eyes widened. His nostrils turned red. His face became pale and fatigued.

A part of me wished everything would return to normal so we could sit a little while longer on the porch and he could teach me about the three simple shifts in perspective he had just mentioned.

But I knew what I had to do. I stood up and put one arm under his elbow and the other around him. "Come on Father. Let's go inside. You've been sitting outside long enough."

What I didn't know as I gently guided him back into his house was that that would be the last meaningful conversation I would have with him.

↺

As he listened to the Young Woman tell her story, the young man reflected on his youth.

He hadn't understood it before, but it was vividly clear to him now. His father had played a pivotal role in helping him achieve his huge success. His father's belief in him had given him the confidence to accomplish what he had never imagined he could accomplish.

He had never imagined himself to be particularly adept at leadership, but his father's implicit belief in his leadership abilities had helped him rise quickly through the ranks. He had never imagined himself to be particularly creative, but his father's implicit belief in his creative abilities had helped him uncover unusually innovative ways to grow his practice. He had never imagined himself to be particularly resourceful, but his father's implicit belief in his resourcefulness had given him the resilience and strength to overcome obstacles that had come his way.

He thought of the times he had bragged to anyone who would listen that he was a self-made man, that he didn't owe anyone anything for all his accomplishments.

How naive he had been!

His mind flooded with images from the past — his father smiling at him encouragingly, his father looking at him lovingly and with complete confidence, his father hugging him proudly.

How could I have misunderstood him so much? How did I end up taking him for granted? How did I get so obsessed with my career that I broke off from him almost completely?

Just then, his father's words echoed in his mind:

"The most powerful way to make a difference in this world doesn't require you to actually *do* anything at all!"

He was so right! Without lifting a single finger, simply by the way he looked at me, simply by his belief in me, Father changed my whole world.

The young man held his breath for a few moments as he composed himself. Nervously, he asked the Young Woman, "So you never had the chance to learn about the three simple perspectives from my father?"

She shook her head no.

They stood together quietly, as though words were no longer necessary to communicate what they were experiencing.

"Imagine," she whispered after a moment. "Imagine a world in which everyone experienced what I experienced with your father! Imagine a world in which each and every one of us was surrounded by people who implicitly believed in our worth and our value! So many more of us would blossom. So many more of us would discover ourselves. So many more of us would reach our true potential. The whole world would change! The whole world would be a different place!"

She clutched her heart. "This feeling, in here, that I received from your father is priceless. It will stay with me forever. How will I ever be able to repay him?"

She reached out and squeezed the young man's hand. In her eyes, he saw a hint of the same kindness and patience he remembered in his father.

He searched her face. He had so many questions. *How am I going to find out about the three shifts in perspective? How am I going to learn to believe in others the way my father did?*

The wind started whistling and the sky collapsed. Raindrops pockmarked the wet fields.

Everyone started scrambling for cover. The orderly line of people before him disintegrated into chaos. And in the chaos, the woman disappeared.

The First Simple Shift

The young man felt a deep ache in his belly. He shielded his eyes with his arm and leaned against a tree, grief wracking his entire body.

Just then, a soft hand gently rubbed his back, and a small voice quivered, "Don't cry. He'll always be alive in our hearts. He meant so much to all of us."

He turned to see a frail older woman, hunched over her walking stick, barely mustering enough strength to soothe him with her hand.

He strained to recognize her. She appeared to be in her late eighties. Her stooped shoulders accentuated her diminutive form. Despite her sagging face and hands, she had eyes that were strong and somehow sad at the same time. Her prominent nose hinted a regal background.

In a small but reassuring voice, she told him, "You don't know me but I know you. Pardon me, but I was right behind you and I overheard some of your earlier conversation."

A smile radiated her craggly face. "Your father was such

a great man. He changed my whole life. I thought you would like to know!"

He wanted to ask, *Do you know anything about my father's three secrets?*

Instead, he asked, "How did you know my father?"

She replied coyly, "I never actually met him. But he *did* change my whole life!"

He nodded, encouraging her to go on.

Her eyes went moist. "Your father gave my son back to me!"

His mind was now racing, trying to connect the dots — *You never met my father but he gave your son back to you? How? When? What did he do?*

But he nodded again silently.

"My son knew your father."

Her face crumpled and she cried softly into a laced handkerchief she'd pulled from her purse.

He placed his hand gently on her back to soothe her. "It's okay, it will all be okay," he said calmly, although he couldn't stand the suspense any longer.

After a while, she cleared her throat and said, "Because of your father, my son's whole life changed. And when my son's life changed, life as I knew it also changed."

She added in barely a whisper, "And now, because of what your father started, the whole world has changed for my sister, bless her soul!"

"What did my father do for your sister?"

She squinted. "You know, I don't think my sister knows anything about your father."

The rain had subsided to barely a trickle. People had loosely started forming a line again.

The young man lowered his head. *How did Father change the lives of people he hadn't met? How did he change the lives of people who didn't know anything about him?*

Guilt clutched his heart. While he had devoted his life to climbing up the corporate ladder, leaving all the people he knew behind in his wake, his father had devoted his life to making the world a better place, touching the lives of people he didn't know.

The Old Lady put her finger tenderly under his chin and looked at his face. "I didn't realize until recently how much we affect the lives of those around us, even people we don't know," she told him.

Her voice breaking, she continued, "Your father affected so many people — including my son. My son, then, affected everyone in his life — his wife, his children, his coworkers, his boss, his employees and me. I am now affecting my sister and my church group. It's a matter of time before my sister affects a whole group of new people!"

She smiled. "Your father started a tiny ripple with my son. Look how far the ripple has come!"

As though she had read his skepticism, she added, "If you had told me just a few months ago, I wouldn't have believed this was possible. Who would have imagined that one person can affect people they don't even know!"

She continued, "I did a few calculations on the way here today." Her bony fingers moved as though punching the digits on a small calculator. "Suppose each of us affects just nine people. Suppose each of us affects these nine people in such a way that *each of them* affects *another* nine people each. And suppose, in this way, every individual affects *another* nine people *each*.

"Assuming that each time we are affecting nine *new* people, by the time we are just ten tiers deep, we will have collectively changed the lives of nearly half the people on this planet!

"Imagine! Three billion people! We will have literally touched enough people to change nearly the whole world!"

She paused to collect her breath. "Every individual has the power to change the world! That is the legacy your father left behind for all of us!"

The young man rubbed his temples. So many questions were buzzing through his mind, he wasn't sure where to start. *How is all this possible? How can one person affect so many?*

Finally, he asked, "How did your son affect your life?"

The Old Lady studied his face for a moment. "Do you

have a little time? I'd be happy to tell you, but first I have to give you a little background."

He nodded eagerly.

She looked up and asked, "Do you have any idea what it is like to be old?"

He saw her hands were trembling. Knowing instinctively they were trembling with pain, not the damp cold, he gently placed his hands over hers.

She continued, "All the people near and dear to me are gone. My husband passed away years ago. Most of my brothers and sisters have since joined him. Those that are still alive are bed-ridden or incoherent or thousands of miles away."

"I live alone now," she said, exhaling. "The loneliness has sometimes been unbearable."

Wiping a tear from the corner of her eye, she went on, "My children are fully grown. They are scattered all over the country. They have lives of their own — family, jobs, friends. I have one son who lives only about a hundred miles away. But I rarely see him. He has a busy life — wife, career, kids. So many things that demand his attention, he hardly has any time for me. I had started wondering if I mattered to him anymore."

He massaged her hand gently. "I'm sure you matter to him very much."

Lowering her voice, her words slow and deliberate, she agreed. "Yes, intellectually, I know that I matter to him.

Once I had to be rushed to the emergency room. The moment he heard about it, he dropped everything and rushed to my side. He appeared shaken.

"But things soon went back to the way they were. He was devoured once again by demands from all directions."

Her chest heaving, she continued, "One day, I noticed that things had somehow changed with my son. I couldn't quite put my finger on what. He wasn't doing anything different when he was with me. He wasn't spending any more time with me. He wasn't calling or visiting any more frequently. But I noticed that, somehow, every moment he spent with me felt more fulfilling, more gratifying, almost magical." Touching her chest softly, she added, "In here!"

Her voice now became a little wobbly. "Even our brief weekly phone calls had somehow become more precious.

"At first, I was afraid to ask him what had changed. I was afraid of breaking the spell. It literally felt like a spell had been cast over us. A spell that had changed everything.

"But one day, after several months had gone by, and the spell still hadn't been broken, I told him how happy I was. How I didn't feel so lonely any more. How I really treasured our phone calls and our visits.

"That's when he told me about the day he met your father! That's when he told me about the day your father shared a little secret with him!"

She looked at the young man and her face lit up. "Let me tell you what my son told me about that day …"

I am the Old Lady's Son

The first time I saw Father, he was surrounded by nearly a dozen kids, including two of my own.

It was one of those Friday-night family get-togethers that is the hallmark of small towns. And Father was the center of the kids' attention.

I was staying for the weekend with my family at the only bed and breakfast in town — my wife's attempt to get me away from my hectic schedule in the city.

But the moment she dropped out of sight, lost among the parents hovering over the appetizers, I glued myself to my cell phone.

First, I called my secretary back at the office.

Next, I made my obligatory weekly call to my widowed mother. I love my mother dearly but lately it seemed like every phone call with her ended in a frustrating tug-of-war. She didn't want the call to end. I, on other hand, was eager to move on to my next call.

It was when I was on hold with my third call that I started scanning the community hall, and my eyes gravitated toward an older gentleman dressed in a slightly-tattered sweater and faded khaki slacks. Although his skin looked pale, his face beamed when he smiled, and it seemed like he was smiling all the time. Even from a distance, I could hear an unusual vibrancy in his voice.

His eyes, slightly sunken though they were, bounced from child to child. And if I wasn't mistaken, his hands were moving in unison with his eyes, first touching one child briefly, then shaking the next one's hand, next ruffling another's hair, then caressing someone's cheek, on to tickling the next child's ear lobe.

For their part, the kids danced and pranced around him energetically. They seemed to be mesmerized by this individual who was at least two generations older. Even though it felt completely impossible and also entirely illogical because of the sheer number of children, I had the uncanny feeling that he had forged a special connection with each child.

Pulling my mouth away from my cell phone, I asked a woman passing by, "Who is that man?"

She turned to look proudly at the old man. "He is the light of our town. We call him Father."

I was eager to learn more about this unusual individual and an opportunity presented itself when the gathering started to wind down. I noticed a few people discussing how to get Father back to his home, and without a moment's hesitation, even though I was exhausted after a long day, I volunteered. At the time, I had no clue that I had just made one of the most pivotal decisions of my life. What followed was truly memorable — a conversation of enlightenment and transformation, of love and liberation, of perspective and wisdom.

I seated Father in the passenger seat next to me, while my wife and kids huddled in the back seat.

As I started the car, I noticed that my kids had edged to the front of their seats, as far forward as their seat belts would allow. My son was speaking so fast, I started worrying that he would soon run out of breath. My daughter watched with round-eyed amazement.

As I shifted my gaze to Father, I finally saw firsthand the genuine interest he had in my kids. I could hear his labored breathing. But I also sensed that every breath he took was for my kids.

Father's attention didn't waver even for a moment from my kids. He asked them about their life, their school, their teachers, their sports, their hobbies, their vacations, their pets. Even though my son, who loves to talk, was answering most of the questions, he divided his attention equally between both my kids.

He was sitting at a slight angle, looking over his shoulder at the seat behind him, his eyes moving gently back and forth between my son and my daughter.

I started getting a sense that neither my kids nor Father were aware that my wife and I were right next to them.

At first, I felt a twinge of jealousy. *How can this complete stranger hold the attention of my kids for so long?*

I tried to dismiss it as just a novelty. *After all, he is new, he is different,* I told myself.

I glanced at my wife in the rearview mirror and I could tell that even she was riveted by this enchanting individual.

This slightly shriveled old man sitting beside me simply had a special way with people. It was charisma, a quiet power unlike anything I had ever seen before.

And then I realized with a near panic that, if I wanted to learn the secret of his charismatic power, I would have to muster up the courage to ask him soon because I was about to drop him off and I might never see him again.

After some time, the conversation between Father and my kids seemed to subside. I glanced over my shoulder and noticed my son nodding off, his sister curled up beside him. They looked exhausted and deeply satisfied at the same time.

The day was finally catching up with them, I realized. We had started the three-hour drive to the countryside almost immediately after they had returned from school.

I looked at the clock on the dashboard and was surprised to see that it had only been five minutes since we had left the community hall, though it felt like it had been much longer.

From the corner of my eyes, I noticed Father looking at me. In soft tones, so as not to disturb the kids, he started asking me about my life, my parents, my career, our home, our family life.

As I answered his questions, I had the strange sensation that Father was totally fascinated by everything I had to say. Although this was by no means the first time I had shared the story of my life with someone else, it was certainly the first time I'd felt that every detail of my life was of paramount importance.

I glanced once again at my wife in the rearview mirror and the expression on her face told me she was both amused and surprised I would open myself up so completely to a person I'd just met.

It was in the midst of one of Father's questions that something clicked inside me and I understood the source of his charisma. Our culture teaches us that charisma comes from drawing, even inspiring, the attention of others to yourself. That being charismatic involves grandiose gestures and good looks and endearing characteristics.

That's incorrect.

That evening, driving down a pitch-dark, two-lane country road, I realized that charismatic people are not those who deliberately draw attention to themselves. Rather, they are people who shower their *own* attention completely on others, and in this way, indirectly and effortlessly, capture the attention of everyone around them.

The mesmerizing power of this simple, unassuming old man lay in the sheer simplicity and the true completeness of his attention, first on the nearly dozen kids in the community hall, then on my kids in the back seat, and finally on me seated by his side.

After a little while, instead of answering his next question, I asked him if I could ask him a question of my own.

He nodded with a kind smile, his gaze holding steady on my face.

"I've been fascinated by how you give each and every individual your undivided attention. I've been even more fascinated by the reaction of all those individuals. Everyone is just riveted. I was wondering if you would teach me how you do it?"

He smiled as though he was expecting the question. "There's nothing to do," he told me. "It's actually quite simple. You start with a deep belief that each and every individual is special."

I nodded pensively. I had personally witnessed Father treating each kid as special. But there was something that wasn't quite clicking for me yet.

"You must meet so many people, just like you did today. How do you do it when you are being torn in a thousand different directions? When there's so little time — and so many people?" I asked him. "There's only one of you!"

Father looked at me for a few minutes. Then, he observed, "I don't get sidetracked by how little time I have. Instead, I focus on how to make the most of what time I have with each and every individual."

He smiled. "As a culture, we're so obsessed with how little time we have that we fail to make the most of what time we do have."

He allowed me a moment and then he added, "We're so busy existing, we're not really living.

"We spend every moment thinking about what we're going to do in the next moment. When we're with our kids, our mind is at the office. When we're in the office doing one task, our mind is on the next task. When we're supposedly listening to our spouse, we're actually thinking about what we're going to say next. We're always thinking about the *next* thing we have to do or the *next* person we have to talk to."

My stomach churned with self-recognition — and guilt.

He went on. "Our society is so obsessed with managing time that we've forgotten what's important about time. When our focus is on *managing* time, when we're constantly multi-tasking, we think we're becoming more effective, but in reality, we're becoming ineffective.

"We think we're making things better, but in reality, we're making them far worse. That's because the person we're with immediately senses that our attention is everywhere but on them. We are diminishing their worth when what we should be doing is *recognizing* their worth.

"When we don't focus our attention on the people around us, why should they focus their attention on anything we say? When we don't value them, why should they value us?

"The end result is the people on whom we rely for support become less and less engaged with everything we do or say. And without their full-hearted support, we become more and more ineffective."

I threw up my hands in a mock gesture. "You've convinced me. How do I get started?"

"With a simple shift in perspective."

"Did you say a shift in perspective?"

"Yes. Stop obsessing about how little time you have. You will *never* have more time than you need. You will *always* have far more to do than you have time available. That's just the nature of things."

"I never thought of it that way."

"Focus instead on making the most of every moment. Make every moment count. Make every moment a symphony. Treat each moment as though it is the most important moment of your entire life. In every moment, create the biggest impact. In every encounter with another human being, treat every moment together as though no one else in your whole world is more important."

"Every moment?"

"Yes, every moment! Whether you're talking to one individual or you're in a room full of over a hundred individuals. Make every moment with every individual special — even if that moment is for just an instant, for just a nanosecond, for just the blink of an eye."

"What else?"

"That's it! Just this simple shift in perspective and every thing you do as a result will sparkle. Even the briefest of encounters will sparkle. You won't need to say a single word, and yet you'll communicate to others how special they are. You will make a huge impact on the world. You will change lives."

He sat silently for a moment, then added, "You'll change your own life as well. You'll become far more effective with everything you do. You'll feel far more fulfilled with everything you do. You'll make your whole world better."

I took my eyes off the road for a second and glanced at him. "May I ask you another question?"

He nodded encouragingly.

"You said to look at every individual as though every individual is the most important person in the world. What if it is not in your makeup to think of other people as important?"

When I glanced at him again, I could tell he was expecting this question.

"I can tell you a simple but powerful way to get started."

"I'd be grateful."

"Whenever you are with another person, whether for a nanosecond or for several minutes, look into their eyes and focus on remembering everything about their eyes — the color, the shape, the length of their eyelashes. Look at every little red streak in the whites of their eyes, see their shape, see their size. Stay focused on their eyes until you're sure you can recount every detail."

"That might be a bit awkward," I protested.

"Everything is awkward the first time."

I glanced at him again. "What will happen when I do this?"

"They will sense that your attention is nowhere else. This will make them feel special. They will feel drawn to you. They will just soak in your undivided attention. That's when your interaction will move to a completely new level. You will start feeling a mutual connection, a bond. You will start seeing that the other person is mirroring your attention back to you, that they're actually listening to everything you're saying. You will find it getting easier and easier to communicate your point of view.

"And once you experience that, you will never want to

go back to looking at another person in the old way again. Before you know it, this new way of looking will become a part of who you are. It will become second nature. And each time you encounter another person, you will make the world a slightly better place."

I blinked as I recalled my weekly phone calls to my mother. All these years, I had blamed my mother for the frustrating nature of our calls. In that moment, I realized I was the real culprit. Even before mother could answer the phone, I'd be scheming ways to end the call, to escape her unspoken demand for more quality time.

Will I ever be able to heal that relationship? I wondered.

Noticing my sudden quiet, Father observed, "Something's bothering you."

I looked at him silently.

"Don't worry," he said. "Once you start looking at everyone in your life with this new perspective, everything will change. Your inattention in the past will be forgiven and your future will blossom."

↺

The Old Lady took a step back and cleared her throat. "Everything changed between my son and me after that weekend. Of course, I didn't understand how or why until much later when I asked him."

Touching her chest softly, she looked into the young man's eyes. "Today, thanks to your father's influence, I feel completely loved by my son. I feel I matter. Just a few minutes with him and I feel ten feet tall! And look at me!"

She pointed to her frail body, barely five feet tall.

She straightened herself as much as she could. "I'm here to pay my last respects to the man who gave my son back to me and who, after all these years, helped me see my long-lost sister in a whole new light — and taught all three of us a whole new way of looking at the world."

She placed her hand on the his wet cheek and wiped his tears away. "Stand proud. Your father's memory will live with us forever!"

With that, she hobbled away.

The young man tried to shout "Wait," but his voice was trapped in his throat.

Tears welled his eyes as he recalled the last time he had seen his father.

They had been standing at his father's doorstep, saying their goodbyes.

The neighbor's dog had been barking. Across the street, an electric saw had been buzzing. Down the street, a few neighborhood kids on skateboards had been filling the air with their high-pitched screams.

Through the din and distraction, his father's attention had remained riveted on him, following his every move.

He had felt like royalty receiving a grand farewell. The center of the universe. Ten feet tall — just like the old woman had described!

Why did I drift away from Father when so many had gravitated towards him?

His insides crumbled as he realized that his father's secret — this simple shift in perspective — had always been in front of him, but he had been too blind to see it.

If he had been too blind to see this one shift in perspective, perhaps the other two shifts in perspective had always been in front of him as well, but he had been too blind to see them. Perhaps all he had to do was search his memory and he would recognize the other two perspectives all on his own.

But his mind was too numb from the emotions of the day and he came up blank.

He looked up hopefully at the line of people before him and moved forward.

The Second Simple Shift

An excited voice called out, "There you are! I've been looking all over for you!"

The young man turned to the direction of the voice and saw a middle-aged man in blue overalls rushing toward him.

"He was sure you would come," the middle-aged man said, extending a callused hand forward. "You look exactly like your picture!"

"You have a picture of me?"

"Yes! Your father gave it to me so I'd be sure to recognize you." Almost as an afterthought, he added, "Oh! Let me introduce myself. I'm the gardener and the general handyman and go-to-guy at the only bed and breakfast in this beautiful town."

The young man studied the weathered face of the Gardener. "My father gave you my picture?"

"Yes!" the Gardener smiled. "He wanted to make sure you were comfortable when you got here. He didn't want you to be tired or inconvenienced in any way. I've set aside a nice suite for you." Looking around the young man, he asked, "Where's your luggage? Let me take it to your room for you."

The young man felt tears. "Father didn't want me to be inconvenienced today?"

The Gardener nodded. "He knew you were busy with your career. But he also knew you would break away from everything and come here right away if anything ever happened. He made me promise ten ways from Sunday that I would make sure you were comfortable."

The young man's voice choked. "Father really loved me."

"He thought you were pretty special!"

The young man squeezed his eyes shut, trying to stop the tears.

The Gardener said gruffly, "Oh, now look what I've done. Your father didn't want you to be hurting or crying. He wanted you to rejoice in his life, not mourn his death."

The young man shook his head and murmured to himself, "I spent so little time with him!"

The Gardener nodded and shut his eyes. After a deep long breath, he said, "There is a way you can make up for lost time."

"How?"

"I learned it from your father."

The young man studied the Gardener's sun-streaked face, his dark eyes, his cracked lips.

The Gardener fiddled with the loops in his overall for a moment. When he looked back up, his eyes were glistening. "Maybe I should start at the beginning."

The Gardener whispered, "Your father gave me a totally new perspective on life."

His lips trembled as though he were deciding whether to say more. Then he sighed. "Before I met him, I used to be depressed about my whole life. My relationship with my own dad was completely destroying me. I hated my dad! I hated him like I've never hated anyone! I wished he would just die!"

The young man searched the Gardener's eyes, encouraging him to go on.

The Gardener drew a deep breath. "My dad was nothing like your father. My dad was ..." And then his face crumbled.

The Gardener looked up at the sky. The young man followed his gaze. The rain had stopped but the clouds looked low, dark, heavy, ready to burst again.

The Gardener resumed his story. "My dad used to be a travelling salesman. A successful one, I might add. Unfortunately, he got into the habit of drinking to while away his time when he was alone in strange towns. But then, before we knew it, his drinking took on a life of its own and became a habit. As he spent more time drinking and less time selling, his commissions started dwindling. Which made him turn to the solace of alcohol even more.

"I still remember the family trying to make do, adjusting to the reduced income, living on welfare checks. Sometimes, mom would have just ten dollars in her purse and we didn't have the faintest clue where the next meal was coming from.

"I still remember Christmas. We would celebrate it a week after everyone else. We'd wait until one of our neighbors had discarded their tree. We'd scavenge the neighborhood for discarded trinkets and wrapping paper and ribbons."

A tear rolled down the Gardener's face. "They say adversity draws people together, making them more resilient, more resourceful. But adversity tore our family apart.

"It wasn't too long before dad started staying out late practically every night and coming home drunk. He'd tramp right into our bedrooms at three in the morning, kick our shoes loudly across the room to wake us all up, yell foul language at the top of his lungs, slap us if we didn't get out of bed fast enough.

"We'd be groggy and crying and he'd march us all into the living room, completely ignoring our tears, loudly commanding us to remain in single file. Then, he'd randomly pick on one of us, and ..."

The Gardener put both hands to his face and his voice

thinned. "I remember one night when he decided to pick on me. It had been my turn that day to do the family laundry. But he didn't like how I'd done it. He yanked all the clothes and linens from all the closets and threw them into a huge heap on the living room floor. Just like that. A whole day's work ruined.

"Then he commanded me to re-fold every item and put it carefully back in all the right drawers and closets so that everything was perfectly lined up and looked like we had just walked into a department store.

"If I didn't fill a drawer properly, he'd empty that entire drawer and make me start again.

"This was my childhood. I was so out of my wits, I was afraid that one day I wouldn't be able to contain myself any longer and I would hit him. I lived with this terror for years. Looking back, I'm not sure how I survived it."

The young man couldn't contain himself any longer. He leaned over and hugged the Gardener.

The Gardener pulled himself together and, between sobs, continued. "Eventually, mom passed away — a helpless, weary woman. Soon after, my brothers and sisters scattered. Every once in a while, if I can locate them, I call them. They are all bitter, lost souls — either addicted and don't know it, or in rehab.

"Dad now lives in a senior citizen center six hundred miles away. No one calls him. No one cares.

"Every year, I feel guilty around the holidays, so I visit him for Thanksgiving. Every year, I swear it will be the last time. He makes me feel so miserable, so small, so worthless, even though we both know I'm doing him a favor. He has no one in his life now.

"This past Thanksgiving, I had absolutely made up my mind that I wasn't going to see him again. I said to myself I didn't have to put up with him any more. It's a good thing I talked things over with your father!"

The young man knew that one more layer of his father's secret was about to unfold.

The Gardener continued. "This past Thanksgiving was the best I've spent with my dad in my entire life. I still can't believe it!

"If one dad and his son, who have hardly talked to each other all their lives, can find a way to connect and communicate, then there is hope and inspiration for everyone — Everyone! There is hope for anyone who has ever been in a relationship that has become estranged."

His face glowed. "Your father was right, you know. This is how we can all make the world a better place. I'm so grateful I had that talk that afternoon with your father …"

I am the Gardener

In all the time I've known Father, the one thing I've come to admire most about him is his ability to make each and every one of us feel special and worthwhile.

I'm just a gardener, an ordinary handyman. But I've often found myself sitting in his home side-by-side with a well-dressed executive in a designer suit, someone who obviously makes nine or ten times what I make in a year — and he will not only treat both of us with equal respect and dignity, he will make sure both of us feel equally extraordinary.

This is a man who walks his talk, who lives what he believes. And his belief is elegant in its simplicity: Each and every human being has a special purpose, a unique value in this universe.

Father's belief is so deep, it is the cornerstone of everything he does.

One example. He never gives advice unless he is specifically asked for it.

At first, I couldn't understand why. So one day, I decided to ask him.

He explained that whenever you give unsolicited advice, you essentially put yourself up on a pedestal — and diminish the worth of the other person.

I had to think about that for a while. But when I finally got it, I was completely floored. What a refreshing and deep *respect* for others.

I admired his philosophy but there was a question bubbling inside me. "If you won't teach us, how will we learn what we need to learn?" I asked him.

His eyes crinkled as he smiled. "Most people learn by observing. They assimilate what's working. If there is anything for me to teach others, the best way for me to do it is by living it, being it, breathing it."

I tilted my head. "What if someone doesn't quite get it through assimilation?"

"Some people learn by osmosis. Others need a wake-up call."

"A wake-up call?"

"Like a crisis. Or the threat you'll lose something you value. For example, divorce. Death. Losing your job. Going bankrupt. Such events often wake us up to learn what we need to learn." He shut his eyes. "You can't force feed people into learning. People learn best when they are ready."

I had one more question. "What if I approached you myself and asked your help with a problem?"

Father looked at me tenderly. "You have a problem?"

"I might!"

He put his hand gently on my shoulder. "If you came to me with a problem, I will help. But I won't give you *the* answer. Because my answer would be strictly that — *my* answer. An answer that works for me may or may not work for you.

"So, I will sit beside you and we will both look at your problem together. If I can, I will try to help you look at the problem from a slightly broader perspective. Our goal will be that with this broad perspective, you will not only be able to come up with the answer that works best for you, but more importantly, you will be able to find the answers to any future such problems on your own."

Imagine a world in which there were more people like Father, driven not by the ego to impose their own views on others, but rather by the belief that others are worthy enough to think things through on their own!

One day last October, I approached Father. "I've been seriously considering not visiting dad this Thanksgiving. What do you think?"

He already knew about my childhood traumas so I didn't need to elaborate.

He turned to look at me. "Let me ask you a question."

"Yes?"

"It may not be that pleasant."

I braced myself. "Go ahead. I'm ready."

"There are three hundred and sixty four days every year between Thanksgivings. You don't see your dad during any of those days. Does that bring you any peace of mind?"

I stared at his liver-spotted hands. "I'm not sure I understand what you mean."

"Think about it. During those three hundred and sixty four days between visits, although you don't see him, don't you still feel anger, rage, frustration? Right now, aren't you feeling anxiety, indecision, consumed? Even though you are physically separated from your dad, do you ever really stop thinking about him? Isn't he nearly always there in your mind, just under the surface of your consciousness?"

My head started pounding. It was true, of course. But I wasn't sure I was quite ready to hear it put into words so explicitly.

He continued, "It has been my experience that you can never really separate from another human being. Maybe you can from a stranger, or from someone you know only in passing. But never from someone you've known for a while.

"Once a relationship has been established, that relationship can never be broken. Once your paths have crossed in a meaningful way, you remain connected forever.

"You might pretend this is not true by creating a physical distance between each other. You might think that once you are separated physically, you are done. The problem is you can separate physically, but never mentally. The voices in the head never go away. In fact, they often become more vicious than before. Sometimes they completely consume you."

My chest felt empty as though every ounce of emotion had been drained out of me.

How could I argue with him? Truth always has a certain ring to it. You may not be able to define it. You may not be able to describe it. But you always recognize it when you hear it.

I hunched. "It is so painful to confront this."

He massaged my shoulder gently. His hands felt shaky and bony, hardly any flesh left on them. At the same time, they felt warm, supportive, paternal.

I suppressed a nervous laugh. "Are you suggesting I should be seeing my dad more frequently?"

"How frequently you visit your dad — or whether you visit him at all — that's a decision you will have to make on your own. But not now. Later."

I scratched my head. "Why later?"

"In order for both of you to be at peace with whatever decision you make, you must first make a slight shift in perspective."

"A shift? In perspective?"

"Yes. Think of it this way. In every decision you make, in every action you take, you either make the world a better place or a worse place."

"I don't understand."

"Right now, everything you're doing with your dad is making things worse. Inside, you are brimming with anger. You are consumed with guilt and indecision. For three hundred and sixty four days a year, all this keeps eating at you from the inside out. On Thanksgiving day, you visit your dad with the false hope that things will get better. But the reality is you have an untenable situation. The way things are, things can never get better. Only worse.

"If you want to make things better — for your dad and for yourself — you must first make a shift in perspective."

Father tilted his head. "May I ask you another question?"

"You think I'll be able to handle it?"

"Of course!"

"Okay, go for it!"

"This question is not as painful as the previous one. But it *is* more difficult."

"I've been warned."

"In all the things your dad has done to you over the years, first terrorizing you as a kid and then mocking you as an adult, do you believe he really wanted to hurt you?"

I sat up. "What type of question is that?"

"I warned you it was going to be difficult."

I sat there, fretting and fuming. A part of me stubbornly refused to deal with the question.

"Do you think your dad meant you harm?" Father asked me softly.

"You tell me! Look at the damage he's done to me over the years!"

"I know," he conceded, "but afterwards, when he is sober, do you think he wishes he could have undone what he did?"

"Then why is he still so cruel?"

Father touched my hand. "Have you considered the possibility that he wants to change but he simply doesn't know how?"

"He's old enough to have figured it out!"

"Age usually has no relationship to what people know and understand."

I stared at him with disbelief, but I couldn't deny his point.

He continued. "Look at your dad. Despite his age, he hasn't been able to confront his drinking. How could he possibly be equipped to undo the damage he's done to you?"

I felt a tear building. I quickly brushed it off. "Why are we talking about this? Are you trying to make me feel sorry for him? It's not going to work."

Father shook his head no.

"Are you trying to tell me I should forget what he's done?"

Again, he shook his head no. "It will probably be difficult to forget it. And you certainly don't want to condone it."

I felt so overwhelmed, I squeezed my eyes shut. "Are you saying I should forgive him?"

"That's a choice you will have to make later. Right now, all I'm talking about is a slight shift in your perspective."

I wrinkled my forehead with frustration. "You keep saying that. But I'm not sure I'm getting it."

"The reason you're struggling with all these decisions — whether to forgive your dad, whether to forget what he did, whether to see him again — is because you haven't *first* shifted your perspective. You have the cart before the horse. Shift your perspective and it won't be such a struggle anymore."

Father looked meaningfully at me for a few moments and resumed. "One of the things I've learned over the years is that most people aren't who they first appear to be.

"They might appear on the outside to be strong and secure, perhaps egotistical, perhaps arrogant, even powerful. They might be accomplished in life, or hold a position of stature. They might look like they have it all together.

"But peel away their mask and look a layer deeper and you'll see all the human frailties and needs. Look past what you first see and you'll see pain, even turmoil, inside.

"You'll see that everyone — *everyone!* — has worries. Fears. Anxieties. Desires. Obstacles. Insecurities. Confusion. Indecision. Denial. Shame. Guilt.

"You'll see that everyone has needs. Goals. Dreams. Broken dreams. Aspirations. Unfulfilled aspirations.

"And you'll see that nearly everyone believes that no one else has it as bad as they do."

I blew out my breath and tried to keep my voice calm. "Are you saying that as tough and angry as my dad comes across, he is really hurting inside?"

Father nodded. "He probably feels unlovable. Powerless. Discarded by society. Left behind."

Leaning forward, Father added, "There's more. Scratch this layer and go one layer deeper and you'll invariably see a person who really wants to do good, a person with an infinite potential to shine."

I backed away from him, shaking my head. "I'm not sure I agree with that!"

He closed his eyes. "The vast majority of people in this world want to do good, they want to matter in this world. When you look deep within them, when you understand their inner motivations, you'll see that their tactics might be ill-advised, but they're trying to right some wrong, they're trying to get some justice. In their mind at least, they're doing good.

"At their core, most people usually have something good about them, something worthwhile, something admirable."

I let my head drop. "Then why do they do such harmful things?"

"Sadly, their potential to do good is buried deep under years of worry, fear, shame, guilt, anxiety and suffering. They live a life of increasing misery because they don't know how to dig themselves out of their mess."

I looked at him blankly.

He sighed. "There are many people in this world who want to do the right things but they simply don't know how. What do you suppose their life is like?"

I shrugged. "I don't know. Why should I care?"

Father moved toward me. He held out his hand. "I don't know your dad, but my guess is he is drowning inside in guilt and shame and sorrow. As miserable as he has made your life, his own life I'm sure is far more miserable."

It felt as though a light had clicked on inside my brain. Father had given me a whole new insight into my dad. Yet, despite my new clarity, questions kept popping into my head. "I'm still confused about exactly what I'm supposed to do."

"That's the best part. You have to do nothing. Simply shift your perspective and everything else will follow. Stop focusing on the big, tough exterior. Focus instead on the pain — and the potential to do good — that hides buried inside."

I swallowed hard. "It's difficult to look past the pain he's caused me."

Father looked at me with kind eyes. "You're too focused on yourself and what you've experienced. Take a moment to move your focus away from yourself to him — and to what he's experiencing. Inside."

I scratched my head. "How?"

"Here's one way. Get in touch with your own humanity. Just like everyone else, you too have needs and frailties buried inside. You too are susceptible to the same influences that have caused him to do what he did. Once you see this, you'll be able to see his humanity! You'll be able to see past his exterior and see the pain and potential buried within!"

I chewed on my lower lip. "What's the point of all this? What will it accomplish?"

He curled his hand into a fist and placed it over my heart. "Once you've looked within a human being this way, once you've seen the true depth of his life's experiences, you'll find a big change coming over you. The way you think about him will change. All the emotions that ruled your perspective in the past — the anger, the hurt, the resentment, the disappointment, the contempt, the bitterness, the fear — will be replaced by a desire to understand. The way you talk to him will change. Even the way you sit with him will change."

I sat up. "But won't I be telling him, in essence, that I condone everything he's done to me?"

"Not at all," he replied. "Keep this in mind. What most people want — what they *crave* — is to be seen. To feel understood. To *matter*.

"More often than not, their inappropriate behavior is little more than their unskilled way of saying — *I matter!*

"So when you shift your perspective, what you're really telling him, in so many words, is — *You matter to me. I may not agree with you or what you're doing. But you matter to me enough that I want to understand what you're experiencing.*

"This small shift will make all the difference in how you interact with each other from that point forward."

I rubbed the bridge of my nose. "I'm not so sure about that. Dad's pretty set in his ways. It's hard to imagine him changing in any way."

He smiled. "Don't underestimate the power you have."

"Power? What power? If anything, I feel powerless."

"Don't underestimate the power you have," he repeated. "You are far more powerful than you think."

I looked at Father patiently, waiting for him to elaborate on this new insight.

He began, "The power you have starts with your own perspective.

"When he behaves inappropriately, if you focus on the pain *you* are experiencing, you'll react with hurt and anger. That's like pouring oil over fire. It sets the stage for him to respond with even more intensity. Eventually, your interactions spiral out of control. You soon forget why you were so hurt and angry in the first place.

"If you focus instead on the pain *he* is experiencing inside, you'll react with inquiry and a desire to understand. He will sense that you are at least trying to understand his inner turmoil. He will sense that, instead of hating him or condemning him or discarding him or pitying him or looking down on him, you *see* him. From that point forward, he will be a bit less bitter, a bit less angry, a bit less threatening, a bit less demanding."

Father folded his hands over mine. "You are far more powerful than you think. Don't abdicate your power.

"In every interaction, *your perspective* sets the stage for how the other person responds to you. *Your perspective* determines the quality of your relationships.

"If the other person is whiny, your perspective sets the stage for them to be more whiny — or less. If the other person is acting needy, your perspective sets the stage for them to act more needy — or less. If the other person is controlling, your perspective sets the stage for them to be more controlling — or less.

"Your perspective plays a huge role in your outcome.

"With your dad, your current perspective will only make things worse. If you shift your perspective, you can make the world a better place."

Something wasn't quite sitting right about what Father had said. I asked, "Isn't that a bit of a stretch? How can anything that happens between my dad and me possibly make any difference to the rest of the world?"

He put his hand gently on my shoulder. "When you shift your perspective, you will trigger a change in your dad. That change might be slight, but that change will reverberate through all his relationships with everyone else.

"Maybe he'll growl a little less. Maybe he'll scowl a little less. Maybe, over time, he'll become a little nicer to all the people in his world. Maybe some of these people will notice the change and they will be a little less miserable for having to deal with him.

"Think of all the people whose lives intersect with your dad's. Your siblings, his siblings, his coworkers, and today, all the people who live and work with him at the senior citizen center. All these years, your dad's innate radiance has remained buried under his tough, mean exterior. And just like you, all these people feel bitter and angry about their acquaintance with your dad. And just like you, many of them may have separated themselves physically from him, but they remain unsettled because, like it or not, they still remain *connected* to him.

"By changing how you see your dad, you will have triggered a change for the better for all these people. You will have changed his whole world."

I had more questions. "Once I've shifted my perspective, I know you said I don't have to do anything. But what do I say to him? What if I say something that sets him off again?"

"Don't worry about saying the right thing. Once you've seen his inner turmoil, once you've seen his hidden desire to do good, your frame of mind will be such that it will be almost impossible for you to say anything ineffective. Almost everything you say *will* be effective.

"Remember, your anger and pain will have been replaced by a desire to inquire and understand. And that will frame everything you say to him. Under those circumstances, how could you possibly say anything that comes across as wrong to him?"

I searched his eyes. "And what about all those decisions I have to make? Whether to see him again? Whether to forgive him? Whether to forget about the past?"

"Once you have shifted your perspective, you will be at peace with yourself whatever you decide to do. And he, too, will find some measure of peace.

"That's how powerful this simple shift in perspective is."

I closed my eyes and contemplated for a few moments. "This certainly makes a lot of sense. But I worry it is not going to be easy."

"It may not," he agreed.

I was breathing heavily now. "It sounds simple. But it is definitely not going to be easy."

He gently squeezed my hand. "At first, it might be a bit of a struggle. But only because it's unfamiliar territory. Only because this is something to which you aren't accustomed.

"But I know, from personal experience, if you get over your initial anxiety, if you just give it a try, then before you know it, it will become second nature to you. You won't have to think about it. You will spontaneously see your dad — *and everyone else!* — with this new perspective.

"And once it becomes second nature to you, everything will change." He paused. "You owe this to yourself and you owe this to the world. Don't ever doubt for a moment the power you have within you to change the world."

I rubbed my chin. "Why me? Why do I have to trigger the change? Why does the burden have to fall on me? Why not one of my sisters or brothers? Why not his caregiver at the senior citizen center?"

Father smiled at me tenderly. "This is not about them. This is not even about your dad. This is about you. About who you are. About how you show up in this world.

"Don't ask yourself — *Why doesn't someone else change?* Ask — *When will I shift my perspective?*"

"Don't ask — *Why me?* Ask — *What kind of person am I if I do not help make this world better?*"

This past Thanksgiving, I once again made my annual trek to dad. I used to look at my dad with so much fear and disgust. This time, I saw him as a human being, yes a flawed human, but my one and only dad. I felt an empathy for him that I had never imagined within me.

On previous Thanksgivings, on the drive back home, my eyes would be raging with anger. This time, they were filled with tears.

Yes, we have a lot of work ahead of us. But, for the first time in all the years I've known him, I actually saw dad relax his frown. I actually saw the faint glimmer of a grin.

The whole world is now a better place.

I didn't see Father again until a few days after I'd returned from Thanksgiving. I couldn't wait to tell him about the weekend.

"You were right!" I told him excitedly. "We have far more power than we think we do. This Thanksgiving, I understood the true depth of that power. I learned that I always play a role in how others react to me. I learned that I can change how others react to me with a simple shift in my own perspective."

I leaned closer and added softly, "Thank you, Father, for taking the time to help me understand. Thank you for helping me learn what I would have probably never otherwise learned."

He hugged me warmly. His eyes looked proud. But I also noticed a faraway look in his eyes that I didn't comprehend.

After a moment of sitting in silence, he observed, "In our culture, it is common, when things turn sour with another person, to break away, to run away, to not see that difficult person any more.

"We never stop to consider the huge price we pay — in lost opportunities to learn and grow, in lost momentum, in lost investment — every time we recycle the people in our lives."

↻

The Gardener looked up at the sky. Once again, the young man followed his gaze. The rain threatened to return with a few gentle drops. The young man looked around. The field had puddles everywhere. The trees and bushes were fluttering in fits.

The Gardener glanced at his watch. "Oh! Look at the time! Got to hurry. We're going to have a full house at the Bed & Breakfast tonight. Still have a lot of work to do to straighten out the property. I'll see you later!"

The young man opened his mouth to protest but the Gardener interrupted him. "Don't worry, I'll find you. You won't be hard to find!"

He gave the young man a spirited high five and turned away, slushing his shoes through the wet fields.

A few yards away, the Gardener stopped. He looked back and said, "You're a lucky man! You know that, don't you?

"You had a great Father! My life is better because *he* was in it!"

The young man waved reluctantly. As he slowly lowered his hand and uncurled it, he wished he could have
spent more time with the Gardener. He wished he could
have mined the *third* perspective of his father's secret.

How many people would say that their *life is better
because* I *am in it?*

His head started spinning as again he thought about the
last time he had visited his father.

He recalled being somewhat uptight, a bit irritable, more
than a little short with his father.

But Father hadn't reacted at all to his impertinence and
impatience. Instead, Father had simply regarded the young
man's face with warmth and tenderness and said, "You
seem to be so eager to hurry back. Whatever project you've
left behind at the office must be really important to you.
That's why you're so tense."

With that, his father had pulled him close and held him
lovingly.

He remembered wondering, *How does he know about
my stress and frustrations at the office?*

Now as he watched the Gardener hurrying away, he
understood the source of his father's insight. He understood how that simple insight had transformed a potential-
ly uncomfortable visit to a warm and tender one.

*He always seemed to understand exactly what I was
experiencing.*

I was so used to it, I took it for granted.

He blinked hard as he realized that his father had modeled his secrets — the simple shifts in perspective — for him all his life.

My father lived these secrets. Why didn't I notice them before?

Now that he knew two of the simple shifts, would he be able to figure out the third one on his own?

For a moment, he felt like the tumblers would fall into place. But something was blocking him and he couldn't shake it loose.

He looked hopefully at the sea of faces in front of him.

The Third Simple Shift

The wind blew from the west, swinging the branches on the trees, sprinkling droplets of rain across the young man's face.

As he looked at the crowd before him moving slowly in the snaking line, he felt engulfed in guilt.

He thought about the symbols of success he had collected over the years — the money, the cars, the clothes, the mansion on the hill, but hardly any genuine friends. He thought about the goodwill his father had collected in those years — from hundreds of people.

He thought about the hard work, the long nights, the relentless ambition his accomplishments had required. He thought about how little effort his father's accomplishments had required.

He thought about how all his possessions and accomplishments would be unnoticed and forgotten once he was gone. He thought about how his father's accomplishments were now eternal.

How did I completely misunderstand Father? How did I

completely misunderstand what matters most?

Suddenly, a voice boomed behind him. "Is that who I think it is?"

The young man turned his head and saw a man, a few years his senior, wearing an executive's pin-striped three-piece suit and a huge smile, rapidly approaching him with his hand outstretched.

His face looked somehow familiar. The nose in particular. Where had he seen that nose before?

Slowly, a look of recognition came over the young man's face. "Well, you're a blast from the past!" he exclaimed.

The Executive grabbed the young man's shoulders, then pulled him closer into a hug. "How long has it been?"

"Since you graduated from high school and went away to seek your fortunes in the world!"

"From what I understand, you didn't exactly stick around much longer."

"I graduated three years after you. Then, I left too!"

The Executive sized up the young man. "Looks like things turned out pretty well for you?"

"You don't look too shabby yourself!"

"So. What brings you here?"

The young man hesitated. Nodding toward the line of people before them, he said, "My father."

The Executive lowered his voice, suddenly understanding. "Your ...?"

The young man nodded silently.

"Sorry. I didn't know."

More somberly, the Executive added, "Life intersects in the most unexpected ways, doesn't it? All those years I knew you in high school and I never met your father. Now, all this time, I've known your father and I didn't know you were his son!"

The young man saw a sadness pass over the Executive's face.

The Executive said, "That's what your father used to say. That all our lives eventually intersect."

He paused for a moment and looked off into the wet field behind him. "Your father gave me a second chance on life. He was that mentor that we all wish we had. He helped me gain a broader understanding of the world. My world simply hasn't been the same since I met him."

As the Executive held his shoulders and gazed into his eyes, the young man felt showered in the same kind of radiance he had experienced earlier with the Old Lady and the Gardener.

"I always knew that one day you'd be somebody big," he told the Executive with quiet admiration.

The Executive lowered his eyelids. "I've accomplished things I never dreamed possible. And I couldn't have done it without your father's guiding hand."

"Can I ask you something?" the young man said.

"Yes."

"You said your world hasn't been the same since you met my father. How exactly did he influence your life?"

The Executive thought for a moment. "You're kidding, right? You don't understand your own father's influence? I would have given anything to be in your shoes so I could grow up under the same roof as your father!"

The young man nodded quickly to hide his embarrassment. "Yes, yes, of course. I couldn't have done as well as I did had it not been for my father." After a pause, he added, "But I want to hear your story."

The Executive tilted his head as if to ask why.

"I want to know everything about my father's life. I want to relive every moment," the young man explained. Closing his eyes, he added, "Life ends. Memories last forever."

The Executive began. "Although I eventually did well, I didn't start out so good. I used to be known as the worst manager in the entire corporation. I managed a group of just twelve people but the turnover was embarrassing. Employees would constantly complain about me behind my back. I could tell my boss was getting frustrated. But I guess he must have thought I had *some* redeeming qualities because he sent me to classes on supervision and leadership and effectiveness training. I attended workshops on team-building and emotional intelligence. But nothing seemed to be clicking. After a while, I started getting nervous that my boss would soon give up on me."

The young man contemplated what the Executive had just told him. In sharp contrast to the Executive, the young man had gained a reputation among his peers for being a born leader. "You just have a way with people," his boss had once told him early in his career.

Why did leadership come so naturally to me? he now wondered.

Aloud, he said, "But clearly, everything changed. What happened?"

"Your father happened," the Executive replied. "From the first day I met him, I had this uncanny feeling that he was going to teach me the things I needed to learn. Things I wouldn't learn anywhere else.

"He taught me things that I don't think anybody else is teaching.

"And he has this great way of paring things down to their core, to their essence — making everything really simple.

"But I didn't realize, until much after the fact, how much he had influenced me and my whole life. I learned so much simply by being around him and watching him and listening to him."

In that moment, the young man understood his father's powerful influence on his own life. *I became a natural leader because of Father. I assimilated leadership from him! And I didn't even realize it!*

The Executive smoothed back his wet hair. "Today, as I look back, I realize that your father had a huge influence, not only on my life, but also on thousands of other lives. And most of them don't know the hand your father had in changing their lives."

The young man pursed his lips. "Which people?"

"Everyone who has been in my life in recent years. My wife, my children. My mother certainly. My boss. And all the thousands of employees in the company I now run. The only reason I've been able to influence the lives of all these people is because of your father's influence."

The young man stood quietly for a moment, his lower lip quivering. *Here's another group of people that Father influenced without ever meeting them!*

Aloud, he asked, "Can you tell me about how my father influenced the lives of your employees?"

The Executive nodded. "That started one rainy afternoon, not unlike today …"

I am the Executive

The third time I walked into Father's home, he was hunched over his dining table, finishing a plate of steamed vegetables. As I leaned over and gave him a hug, I noticed his frame felt somehow smaller than before.

"Well," he said, smacking his lips, "what have you brought for me today?"

I extended my bare hands toward him. "I thought your doctor said no more goodies."

With an impish smile, he wagged his finger at me. "Well, have you at least brought me an interesting topic for discussion?"

"Actually, yes. People problems."

He waved his fork at me. "People. Problems. Those two words don't belong together in the same sentence."

I mulled that over for a minute. "But," I protested, "I do have people problems and I need help."

He responded with a laugh. "You're right about that! If you have people problems, you do need help. A lot of help!"

Ignoring his double-entendre, I forged forward. "I have this employee who is getting to be a real problem. Everyone wants me to fire him. My boss wants me to fire him. My peers want me to fire him. My other employees want me to fire him."

He raised a bushy eyebrow at me. "I thought you told me last time that your boss was seriously concerned about the high turnover in your department?"

"Yes, but this particular employee is so obnoxious, everyone wants him out!

"What makes him so obnoxious?"

"I don't know."

He contemplated a piece of broccoli on his plate. "Of course you know. Think."

"How would I know?"

He shot me a look. "Take your time. There's no hurry. If you think about it, you'll find you already know the answer.

"Sometimes the most important things hide in plain sight until you decide you're ready to see them."

I looked at the open window behind him. The rain was slanting in, wetting the sill. "I think he's territorial," I said. "He doesn't like anyone messing with anything that's his. He's like a bulldog. Anytime someone touches any-thing he considers his, he literally chases them away, growling, protesting. Most people avoid him rather than deal with him."

Father grinned at me. "In other words, he'd be perfect for guarding something valuable at your company? No one would ever be able to touch the stuff unless he agreed!"

I sighed. "I suppose that's one way of looking at it."

He shifted his weight in his chair. "That's the *only* way of looking at it."

Moving his face closer to mine, he asked, "Tell me, is there a part of your company that could benefit from some really tight security? Like, for example, accounting … quality assurance … shipping … purchasing … warehousing?

At the mention of warehousing, I clenched my lips tightly.

"He works in warehousing, doesn't he?" he said before I could. "And, let me guess, you also happen to have a serious security issue in your warehouse?"

I nodded my head reluctantly, a bit miffed that he had homed in my problems so easily. Our warehouse was indeed an embarrassment. Our inventory accuracy was in the toilet. People from all over the company would go into the warehouse and take stuff or move stuff without documenting what they did.

We sat there quietly for a few moments. I returned my gaze to the rain drops wetting the window sill. I wondered what insights I would gain if I could see things the way Father saw them. That's when, with a flash of the obvious,

I knew what I needed to do.

Three months passed before I had the opportunity to return to the small town and visit Father again.

Before I entered his room, I could hear him coughing from the hall. I tried to convince myself that it was my imagination, that his coughing hadn't become more frequent and more violent than before.

When I entered his room, I saw him sitting on his bed, legs dangling from the side, hands clutching the edge of the mattress. His face looked more pale than before, his cheekbones more pronounced. His eyes were closed. The bedsheets were heaped in a mound behind him. I couldn't tell whether he was preparing to sleep or ready to get up.

"How's your territorial employee?" he asked.

I was a little taken aback that he had skipped the usual pleasantries. But his eyes remained closed and I decided I had little choice but to answer him.

"He's doing phenomenally well," I reported. "I put him in charge of the warehouse within days of returning last time. I told him I was expanding his territory to include the entire warehouse — and would he please guard his expanded territory with the same vigor as he guards everything that's his."

I was so excited about what I had to report, I had to pause to catch my breath. "It's the most incredible thing. In just ninety days, he has tightened all security and enforced all the policies and procedures. No one goes into the warehouse unless they're authorized. No one leaves without completing the necessary documentation."

"And how are the inventory records?"

"That's why I'm here. To tell you about it. We just conducted an audit of our inventory records. The accuracy has skyrocketed from fifty percent three months ago to nearly a hundred percent now."

Without missing a beat, he asked, "How is his demeanor?"

"The number of complaints has definitely come down. And I've heard a few compliments about what a big difference there's been in the warehouse. He seems to be in his element."

"He is in his element!" he repeated.

He opened his eyes. "Isn't it remarkable what a simple shift in perspective can do?" His eyes twinkled.

Father winced slightly as he stood up and slipped his feet into his slippers. I hurried to his side to steady him. Shrugging me off, he shuffled to the dining room.

Slowly, he sat down at the head of the table. "It's a good thing you shifted your perspective about this territorial employee three months ago. Otherwise, you would have had no choice but to put him out on the streets by now."

Looking at me from the corner of his eyes, he added, "Instead, now, you're in the company limelight for turning around a problem employee and also, for turning around an untenable situation in the warehouse."

Father gestured to a chair. "Do you see how a simple shift in perspective makes such a world of difference? When you were focused on your employee's weakness, you were ready to fire him. But when you shifted your focus to seeing the strength *hidden* within that weakness, he turned out to be a star employee."

He looked at me meaningfully and added, "And by the way, so did you!"

Pride surged through my entire body. But I shifted silently on my feet because I still had some questions. "This is so simple!" I exclaimed. "Why don't most people see others from this perspective?"

He smiled. "The problem with most people is they are mentally lazy. They take the easy way out and put everything into 'either/or' buckets. Either something is good *or* it is bad. Either a particular characteristic is a strength *or* it is a weakness. In their lazy minds, a weakness cannot *also* be a strength.

"But this is not the reality of life. It is not the reality of human beings. People are multi-faceted. They *simultaneously* have good qualities and bad qualities. They *simultaneously* have strengths and weaknesses. Often, what is a strength in one situation becomes a weakness in another. And vice versa."

Father continued. "When you go through life with an 'either/or' perspective, when you go through life pigeon-holing people, you don't really experience life at its fullest. You go through life as though you have just half a brain. At every turn, you are seriously limited and you don't even realize it.

"You think you're being very effective when you remove someone 'wrong' from your life. But the reality is you become very ineffective because your limited perspective prevents you from bringing out the best in people.

He barely paused for breath. "You end up recycling all the people in your life because almost everyone has *something* 'wrong' with them."

I didn't say anything. It didn't seem necessary.

He seemed quite animated now. "How much simpler can it be? Stop looking for what's wrong with people. Instead, focus your attention on what *makes* them right."

Father exhaled loudly. "When you start looking for what makes people right, you'll realize that their greatest weakness is often the *source* of their greatest strength."

"That's right!" I chimed. Everyone had deemed the territorial nature of my warehouse employee to be his greatest weakness. But it had turned out to be his greatest strength.

Father stood up. He was clearly passionate about the subject. "Every individual has the potential to be infinitely great. But what's really frustrating is that this potential remains inaccessible for most, if not all, of his life. That's because everybody looks at him with their 'either/or' perspective and labels him as good or bad."

Slowly emphasizing each word, he added, "You hold the key to unlocking the potential within everyone around you. All it takes is this simple shift in perspective.

"With this simple shift, you can move everyone from a losing position and *put them in their element*. With this simple shift, you can allow everyone around you to blossom. With this simple shift, you can change the whole world!"

Nodding my head, I sat down. "This is pretty phenomenal," I told him. "I can't wait to start looking at my other employees with this new perspective."

Father was on a roll. He asked, "Do you know what's even more phenomenal?"

I shook my head no.

"This simple shift in perspective will ripple to places you haven't yet imagined."

"Ripple?"

"Yes, ripple. You may not realize it, but with your territorial employee, you started a ripple of change that could very well extend to infinity," he said.

I frowned, not sure I understood.

"This simple shift in perspective will change the dynamics in your entire organization," he explained. "Now, as a result of this success you've experienced with your employee, others will also want to achieve the same success. They, too, will shift their perspective. Instead of hunting for what's wrong with all the people in your organization, instead of trying to fix or fire everyone who is wrong for your organization, they'll focus their attention on discovering what's right about everyone in your organization."

"That would be a fundamental shift in the culture of our organization," I agreed.

"Think of the lives you will change. Instead of discarding people because they don't fit, you will be bringing out the best in people and helping them fit — but not necessarily in the way you originally expected."

I could see Father was quite excited now. His eyes were lit up, his nostrils flared, his cheeks ruddy. In a breathless voice, he continued, "Think of the ripples this will create *outside* your organization."

"Outside the organization? How?"

"As this perspective gets imbedded into your corporate culture, as more and more people within your organization understand the value of this simple shift, they will take it outside your organization — *to their homes*. They will start viewing everyone in their life in a new way."

I interrupted, "I can see that. I know I'm going to look at

my kids in a totally new way."

"Just your kids?"

"My wife as well. My mother, certainly. My friends."

Father took a deep breath. "This simple shift in perspective will change the world for so many."

"They should be teaching this in every school, every college, every corporate education program in the country!" I exclaimed. "Why don't they?"

Father leaned toward me. "Want to play a word-association game?"

I said nothing. We both knew the question was rhetorical.

"I'll name a characteristic that our society says is a liability. In return, you name a situation in which that same characteristic is an asset."

I wasn't sure I was quite ready for such a game, but I tried to hide my uncertainty. "Let's give it a go!"

"Here's the first one. Persnickety about details."

I contemplated that for a moment. "I suppose someone who is persnickety about details would be an asset in accounting. And quality assurance. And, oh yes, maintenance."

"Good! Here's another. An independent individual who is not a team player."

I studied my fingers. After a while, I shook my head. "I'm not sure I'd want anybody who isn't a team player in my organization."

Father let out a sigh. "Then your whole organization would suffer!"

That made something click and I understood what he was driving at. Sitting up straight, I exclaimed, "Of course! An independent thinker would have no qualms about challenging our thinking. He or she would force the rest of us to consider alternatives we wouldn't otherwise consider."

Father nodded. "There would be some extra tension in the team, definitely. But it would be more than offset by the far broader exploration of ideas. Your organization would go to levels far higher than otherwise possible. Such an individual would actually strengthen your team, not weaken it as most people assume."

He went on. "Ready for one more? A stubborn individual."

"I think I'm getting the hang of it. A stubborn individual would be a real asset in making sure a project gets completed on time and within budget. They would be persistent, barrel through all obstacles and simply not take no for an answer."

I thought about it some more. Then I added, "Also an entrepreneur. An entrepreneur moves stubbornly forward even though everyone says the venture will fail.

"Come to think of it, a scientist at the cutting edge must also be stubborn."

He swung back and forth in his chair as he contemplat-

ed what I had said. "Now let's go faster. How about a disorganized individual?"

I raised my eyebrows. "Creative people are often very
disorganized. It's the source of their creativity!"

He nodded. "How about a gabber, a person who loves to
talk?"

"A gabber would be excellent as an entertainer or as a
salesperson or in public relations."

"How about someone who is cold, unemotional?"

I had to think about that one. "How about a job that
requires cold precision? Like a surgeon?"

He laughed. "Yeah, you wouldn't want an emotional surgeon!"

He laced his fingers together. "Yes, you are now ready to
change the world!"

Father looked across the table at me. "I know you are
ambitious, driven and goal-oriented."

I nodded, not sure where he was going with this new line
of thought.

He continued. "Now you have a whole new way to
achieve your ambitious goals. Instead of being ambitious
for the sake of ambition, instead of seeking power for the
sake of power, focus your attention on bringing out what's
right in all the people around you.

"By making this simple shift, you will be surrounding
yourself with people operating at their optimal best. You

will be surrounding yourself with people *in their element.* You will be surrounding yourself with people who become *engaged* in you. And they will take you to heights you never imagined possible. In time, you will look back at your own goals and laugh at them because they were so puny compared to what your optimally performing people will help you accomplish.

"There's more. People who go through life with an 'either/or' perspective are disconnected from the true reality of human beings. No wonder success brings them loneliness, burn-out, disillusionment. No wonder their success is almost always short-lived.

"With this simple shift, you will see the multi-faceted nature of everyone around you. You will see their true nature. In doing so, you will connect with them in the deepest way possible. And you will find your success brings genuine joy, satisfaction and loyalty.

"In changing the world around you, you will have changed your own world as well."

↺

The Executive looked at the young man. "From that point forward, there was no looking back. Before I knew it, I had gained a reputation throughout the corporation for turning 'problem' employees into stars. Instead of wanting to quit my department, now people wanted to be part of my team. As time went on, I started getting responsibility for more and more. And next thing I knew, I was running the whole company."

His voice dropped a notch. "You know, it's wrong what they say. They say that in the world of business, there are only three things that matter — and they are execution, execution and execution.

"That day, I learned from your father that how well you execute starts with who you are and how you see the world. How you see the world governs everything you achieve in this world. How you see the world governs your entire experience of the world — business, personal, spiritual."

The young man nodded with a new sense of clarity. "In the world of business, the three things that matter most are perspective, perspective and perspective."

The Executive looked at the young man closely as though deciding whether to speak. "In *life*, the three things that matter most are perspective, perspective and perspective."

The Executive smiled. "The third simple shift in perspective changed everything for me.

"It changed my relationship with my kids. Before I met your father, I was so determined to make sure they were successful *the way I wanted them to be successful*. I had their futures all mapped out. Which schools they would attend. Which careers they would pursue.

"I had already identified the traits in them that would prevent them from achieving this success. I had hired coaches and trainers to help them fix those traits. After I met your father, I realized that my ambitions for my kids might make them rich and successful, but that they would be miserable, even disillusioned later in life.

"Now my focus is entirely on discovering who they really are, on identifying a path which will bring out what's already right inside them, on uncovering what's right even within the traits society calls wrong.

"Instead of forcing them to become what would make me look great, I focus my attention on bringing out their innate greatness.

"The results have been phenomenal. For example, one of

my children is gathering accolades across the state for her proficiency in music, a field I previously would have never imagined for either child.

"And my son, my dear little son! His school teacher used to complain that he talks all the time, that he talks too much, that all the other kids are constantly complaining about him. Before I understood this third shift in perspective, I used to discipline my son, make him practice listening, rather than talking.

"Today, I realize how wrong-headed that approach was. I've been helping him hone his speaking skills. I've been encouraging him to join his school's debating contests and lately, he's actually brought home a few awards. This year, he's running for Student Body President. He's the front runner. I think he's going to win!"

The Executive paused to wipe the corners of his eyes. "Even my relationship with my wife has changed. Previously, there was a lot of unnecessary tension. You see, I'm adventurous and spontaneous — a man of the world, who lives for the moment, constantly seeks new challenges, always craving new experiences. I love travelling, meeting new people, going to happening restaurants. If I like something, I buy it on the spot. Life's too short to hesitate.

"My wife, on the other hand, tends to be more of a homebody, a bit tight-fisted with money, the kind of person who will wear her clothes even if they are slightly outdated as long as they are not quite worn out.

"For her, the hassles of travelling far outweigh the excitement. She's more comfortable hanging out with the friends she's known since high school. She'd rather labor over the kitchen and eat a home-cooked meal. I don't think I've ever seen her just buy something on an impulse.

"Things between us had heated up to the point that we'd argue every day about how different we are from each other. I was stuck in the mentality that anything different from me is somehow wrong or bad.

"But now, with this simple shift in perspective, I see so clearly how all the ways in which my wife is different from me is actually an asset to our marriage. I see how she brings a rich fullness to my life. I see how I would have been completely broke by now had she not been a tempering effect on my spending ways. I see the value of having loyal, lifelong friends who quickly come to your side in an emergency. I actually now enjoy spending a quiet weekend at home with my family. When I feel the urge to travel and discover new places, we now come with the family to small, out-of-the-way towns like this.

"I never imagined I would, but I have come to see that our differences make us stronger. Everything I thought was so wrong about her is actually so right for our marriage.

"She's so much happier. I'm so much happier. There's joy in our marriage. Our world has completely changed."

The Executive leaned toward the young man and in a secretive voice asked, "Do you know what else has changed our marriage?"

The young man tilted his head, encouraging him to go on.

The Executive continued, "It was that first shift in perspective that I learned from your father. The one about focusing, not on how little time we have, but on making the most of how little time we have.

"With my busy schedule, I wasn't spending a lot of time with my wife. But now that we have shifted our perspective, everything has changed. We both cherish every moment, making the most of every moment together. Our love has become deeper than I ever imagined possible."

The wind picked up, whistling its way through the trees.

The Executive slowly surveyed the countryside around him. "This is where it all started," he exclaimed. Recognition seemed to kindle his eyes and soften his face. "It started right here one Friday night at the community hall in town. I volunteered to drive your father home. I will never forget that drive through the dark countryside."

The young man did a double take. It all fell into place, why the Executive's nose looked so familiar. The regal nose. The Executive was the Old Lady's son.

Barely able to contain himself, the young man recalled something his father was fond of saying.

"Eventually, all our lives intersect. We don't realize it

but we each affect everyone else. And one way or another, we all change the world — for better or for worse."

The young man looked at the Executive with a new sense of connection and recognition. His eyes filled with tears.

A smile radiated the Executive's face, melting a decade off his age. "Today, the whole world is better *because of him!*"

Turning his head toward the sky, he added, "Wherever he is right now, I know your father is changing someone's world — making someone's world a much better place! Who would have thought a few small shifts in perspective could make such a world of difference."

As if in response, the wind subsided — as suddenly as it had picked up its fury.

A sliver of sunshine peeked through the clouds.

The Executive held the young man's hands. "Words couldn't begin to describe how I feel about knowing you and knowing your father. Thank you, my friend, thank you."

The young man nodded and closed his eyes.

The Executive hugged him. After a few moments, the Executive gently pulled away.

The young man heard the sound of the Executive's shoes. He stood there listening to the shoes puddling the wet field until he couldn't hear them anymore.

As he replayed his conversation with the Executive, the young man felt himself brimming with guilt and remorse to the point of overflowing. He had a foreboding that if he didn't calm himself down, he'd start hyperventilating.

How many people did I dismiss from my life because I wasn't willing to look beyond their weakness? How many lives in this world did I destroy because I didn't look for the strength hidden within?

Why did I dismiss my own Father from my life?

I dismissed him because he didn't have the same ambitions I did. I dismissed him because he was different from me!

He felt a tightness in his throat, a shortness of breath, a conviction that his legs were about to cave.

He screwed his eyes shut and in that moment, he began to see his father in a completely new light. *How could I have been so blind? What I saw as his weakness was actually his greatest strength. It was what changed the world for all the people here today.*

He clutched his hands together in a desperate attempt to calm himself. *Why did it take something like this for me to finally understand my father?*

He looked ahead at the crowd before him. *This is my wake-up call. Help me, Father. Help me finally wake up. Help me learn what I needed to learn all these years.*

A New Beginning

The sky changed color again, from gray to blue. The young man felt the warm sun on his forehead. He closed his eyes and inhaled the rich aroma of wet soil.

Suddenly, he snapped his eyes open in disbelief. He sniffed a few times and looked around suspiciously. And then he was sure. Wafting through the fresh country air was the faint but familiar smell of stale body odor.

As if to confirm his suspicion, a squeaking shopping cart rolled toward him on the path paralleling the field.

"Can you spare a dollar?" a gravelly voice asked from behind the cart.

As the the cart wobbled toward him, he heard the click-click of metal against metal, the familiar sound of a wheel out of alignment.

Involuntarily, the young man stepped back.

The shopping cart was overflowing with dirty clothes, tattered cardboard boxes and old tins and cans. Everything in the cart seemed to be colored a different variation of dirty brown.

"Give me a dollar and I'll share a secret with you," the same gravelly voice offered.

The young man wrinkled his nose and turned to walk away. *What is this homeless person doing at my father's funeral?*

"I shared this same secret with your father!" shrieked the voice after him.

This stopped the young man.

Could this homeless person possibly know something more about my father's secret?

He hastily pulled out his wallet, yanked out a dollar and held it out. He saw a tattered glove dart out from behind the cart, clutch the bill, then disappear.

It happened so fast, he couldn't help but stare at his hand.

In the center of his palm, where the dollar was a moment before, he saw a crumpled, yellowing piece of paper. He pulled his hand toward himself and, fingers trembling, caressed the paper open. In faded blue letters, it said —

See
The Intrinsic Worth
of Every Person
You Encounter

The young man remembered his father had said these exact words to the Young Woman.

He remembered her description of that afternoon. A lazy afternoon. On the porch. Afternoon tea. A homeless person with a noisy shopping cart disappearing around the corner.

As he looked up at the scraggly face behind the cart, he recalled his father's words, "I see a unique individual with a significant, special purpose in this universe. With an intrinsic worth and value. For the world and for me."

His mind racing, the young man wondered — *Can I possibly see the same intrinsic worth that my father saw?*

He looked up and gazed at the person peeking at him from behind the cart.

He willed himself to see the person's intrinsic worth, not sure just what he would discover.

He closed his eyes, scrunched his eyebrows, tilted his chin forward and pressed his lips together.

He opened his eyes slowly.

Nothing seemed to have changed.

Frustrated, he glanced once again at the yellowing piece of paper and noticed that there was one fold still left to be unfolded.

Heart thumping, he gently brushed the edge of the paper with his fingers to unfold it. Inside, in the same faded blue writing, it said —

See
The Intrinsic Worth
of Every Person
You Encounter

— Focus, not on how little time you
  have, but on how to make the most
  of what little time you have with
  every person

— Focus, not on what you see on the
  outside of a person, but on the person within — see the pain within
  and see the potential within

— Focus, not on what's wrong with a
  person, but on what makes them
  right — see their strength within
  their weakness

The young man gazed once again at the shape hiding behind the cart. He thought he noticed a nod of the head, barely perceptible, encouraging him to follow the suggestions on the paper.

He nodded back as if to say *I understand.*

He squeezed his eyes shut, held them tight until he couldn't hold them together anymore and then slowly, he opened them again. Nothing seemed to have changed. Everything seemed to be just as it had been before.

He glanced at the first shift in perspective — "Focus, not on how little time you have, but on how to make the most of what little time you have with every person."

He had heard about this perspective from the Old Lady.

He looked across again.

Suddenly, just like that, it didn't seem to matter any more that there was a crowd of people still ahead of him, that he still had to wade his way through the crowd.

Suddenly, just like that, none of the events of the day seemed to matter any more, not his father's death, not the mass of people all around him, not the wet fields, not the cool breeze, not even his own guilt and shame for being blind to his father's influence.

He was overpowered by the feeling that this would be the last time he would be seeing this homeless person. He felt a deep need in his gut to make sure they both cherished this encounter.

He then became aware that only a few seconds had passed since he'd looked up from the paper. But those seconds felt like an eternity. He had a sense that the power of those few seconds would never end.

Again, he thought he detected a slight nod behind the shopping cart. Again, he assumed the nod was encouraging him to follow the suggestions on the paper.

He glanced down to read the second shift in perspective — "Focus, not on what you see on the outside of a person, but on the person within — see the pain within and see the potential within."

This was the perspective the Gardener had talked about.

The young man lifted his gaze to look across, and he felt his eyes moisten and his heart soften. He realized he felt a certain respect and *kinship* toward the life hidden behind the cart, toward this complete stranger who didn't feel like a stranger any more.

He saw a lifetime of struggles, disappointments and aspirations — as though they were all his very own. He saw the fear, the anxiety, the confusion, the uncertainty, the suffering. He saw the innate desire to be happy. And then, he saw the intrinsic desire to be seen and to be loved — and to do good.

The young man closed his eyes and blinked back his tears. *How is it possible to have such a deep sense of another human being?* he asked himself.

When he opened his eyes after a few moments, he noticed the brief nod again. This time, he was sure he'd seen the nod.

The young man looked once again at the piece of paper in his hands. He read the third shift in perspective — "Focus, not on what's wrong with a person, but on what makes them right — see the strength hidden within their weakness."

He looked up again, and somehow, he didn't seem to care any more whether the person before him was a man or a woman, successful or homeless, educated or uneducated, clean or unclean.

A voice whispered inside him — *Why doesn't it matter anymore?*

But he knew the answer wasn't in the least important.

His eyes twitched, his breath quickened as he realized that behind all the grime and the aroma before him was a human being of intrinsic worth.

He felt a pit in his stomach as he recalled his father's words, "The intrinsic worth of another human being is often not immediately apparent. Maybe there's a special time when they will come into your life and change everything. It doesn't matter. All you have to *know* is that the worth is in there, that this is the way of the world."

As he stood there, looking across at the person behind the shopping cart, the young man thought about the kind of person he used to be, the kind of person he had been just a short hour before when he had first stepped out of his car into the rain to join the crowd of people who had come to pay their last respects to his father.

He knew that, had he encountered this same homeless person just an hour earlier, he would have looked right past the person as someone inconsequential, hopeless, useless, nothing.

But now as he looked across, he saw a human being who was pivotal to everything that was happening around him.

He saw a human being who had been instrumental in changing his father's perspective of the world.

He saw a human being who was *the source* of his father changing the world for all the people in his world.

He saw a human being who was key to helping him understand the power every individual has to change the whole world.

He saw a human being with a special purpose and an intrinsic worth.

Tears were flowing down to his shirt. But he was so focused on the person behind the cart, he didn't blink and he didn't wipe his cheeks.

He finally understood why it is so important to be completely aware of the intrinsic worth of every person you encounter. If you aren't aware of it, you won't look for it. If you don't look for it, you won't see it. And if you don't see it, your whole world will change, not for better, but for worse.

You will miss some of the most important lessons life has to teach you.

How many lessons have I missed because I looked past the human being who brought me that lesson?

With a jolt, the young man realized that he had been so focused on looking at the eyes peering back at him from behind the cart, he had completely forgotten about himself.

He felt as though he had stepped into a refreshing pool of cool, blue water where every pain, every anxiety, every need, every distress had been washed away.

If this is how you feel when you recognize the intrinsic worth of another person, I wonder how it feels to the person you are seeing with this perspective?

He looked up. The eyes behind the cart were smiling at him through a rainbow of tears — and he had his answer.

As the moment engulfed him, the young man looked once again at the faded letters on the yellowing paper.

He was struck by the elegant simplicity and the profound implications of the secret.

It all starts with how you see the world, he realized. Change how you see the world and *you will change the world*.

You start by changing your world. You end up changing *the* world.

When you look for the intrinsic worth in a person, you see the truth inside them. You lovingly see them just as they are, without judgment or expectation. You see them as perfect despite their imperfections. You look at them as though they are the most important person in every moment you are with them.

A remarkable thing happens when you look at another person with so much love and so much faith.

Your belief in them infuses them with a deep self-confidence. You open the way for them to bring their true potential to the world.

You make a difference in their life so profound that anything you can possibly *do* for them pales in comparison.

The young man looked at the sea of people moving forward to pay their last respects to his father.

He blinked back his tears as he realized how effortless it is to change the whole world. How one person's influence can ripple out to all of humanity.

When you see the intrinsic worth of other people, it's as though you switch on the light that hides within them.

Some of these people, maybe all of them, will take that light and use it to switch on the light that hides within the people *they* encounter. And then, some of these new people will switch on the light within the next group of people.

In this way, each group of people will change the next group of people and the next group will change the ones that follow.

And in this way, through a chain reaction that extends through eternity, you will have changed the whole world!

For a moment, the young man imagined his father right beside him, the father who had just passed away, the father who had made such a difference in the world that a whole world of people had come to grieve him.

The young man looked into the eyes still smiling at him from behind the shopping cart and silently voiced a gracious, "thank you."

He closed his eyes and whispered a silent prayer to his father —

Thank you, Father, for giving me this wonderful gift. Thank you for always believing in me. Thank you for making the biggest difference one human can make in the life of another.

My life is so much more complete today because of the way you always looked at me.

You were right. It's a gift that costs nothing — yet its impact is priceless and timeless.

Help me, Father, to give this magical gift to everyone I encounter. Help me, Father, to change the world.

The End

The Change Spreads

The young man held his breath as he scanned the room. It had been exactly seven months since that day when he had stepped out into the rain in the small town his father had called home. Seven months since he had learned his father's secret to changing the world. Seven months since he had first experienced the joy and hope that engulfs you when you first change how you see the world.

Seated before the young man were six people.

Six people committed to transform their relationships ... and to spread change throughout the world.

He had just finished telling them about that pivotal day seven months ago in the wet fields.

What he hadn't told them yet was that he was the young man in the story.

The young man looked into the eyes of each person individually. *Do they understand the full significance of the story?* he wondered.

The room was quiet. A few stirred in their chairs, looking at each other nervously to see who would break the silence.

Then, Robin dabbed her eyes and said quietly, as though talking to herself. "So, this is what love feels like?" Her eyes glistened. "Thank you for sharing this with us."

The young man nodded gently. He felt the urge to speak, to clarify, to elaborate. He wanted to spell out the *underlying* lessons of the story. Lessons that had not been obvious to him at first. Lessons that made the shifts in perspective even more urgent.

But he pressed his lips together. *The lessons will be far more powerful if they figure them out on their own.*

His eyes rested on Sandy who was seated across the room. He noticed her divert her eyes, pick a piece of lint off her blouse and flick it away. She began, "All the scriptures and teachings over the years have taught us to *love thy neighbor.* But I've always wondered — how do you love someone you don't like? How do you love someone who is not nice to you?" Her face crumpled. "How do you feel compassion for someone who is abusive to you?"

Nodding to herself, she looked at Jim who was seated on her left and then at Brian on her right. She added, "This helped me immensely with those questions. Thank you."

As if on cue, Jim started rising from his chair. "Love! Compassion! Quite frankly, I don't know what the fuss is all about. There's nothing new here. We already know all this stuff." Pointing his gaze at the young man, he added, "Thank you for the reminder."

The whole room suddenly became very still as all eyes zeroed in on Jim.

B rian pursed his lips and for the first time, the young man noticed how thin his lips were. Brian tilted his head. "He's right, you know. These days everybody is talking about *change*. Everyone is chanting *peace*."

He breathed in. "And everyone is telling us how love will change the world. How compassion will transform the world. How non-judgement and non-violence are key."

He lifted his head and looked at the young man. "There are all these peace rallies and gatherings. Conferences and festivals. Courses on non-violence and loving communication. And the internet is literally brimming with people wanting to change the world."

S andy looked again at Jim. The young man noticed a tenderness in her eyes. "I can't help but wonder," she said softly. "If we all know this already, if we're already talking about it at gatherings and web sites, why's there so little love and compassion in this world?"

Robin nodded. "Why's there so little peace?" she chimed. "Why so many broken homes? Why still so much separation and segregation? And why are depression, addiction and loneliness — all of which stem mostly from troubled relationships — trending upward?"

Todd, who had been observing the discussions quietly, rubbed his chin. "I think the problem is we all think that *we* act lovingly and compassionately, and that it is *everyone else* who needs to learn how to do so."

Robin looked up at the ceiling. "The truth of the matter is we're *all* missing something truly fundamental."

Brian leaned forward to emphasize the point he was about to make. "I agree. The story shows us so clearly that it's time we took a fresh look at how we're trying to change the world."

Jim slid back into his chair.

At the back of the room, the tea kettle began whistling. Tracy, who had been standing by the serving cart, unplugged the kettle and poured herself a cup. Turning to the group, she asked, "Is it just me, or did anyone else notice that the words *unconditional love* and *compassion* were never once mentioned in the story?"

The young man drew his breath, surprised this point had come up so early in the discussion.

Her spoon clinked as she stirred her tea and everyone fixed their attention on her spoon as though mesmerized.

She closed her eyes. "I think it was deliberate. And that's because love and compassion will *not* change the world."

"What?" Brian murmured under his breath.

Tracy opened her eyes. "Love and compassion, the way we traditionally *think* about them, will not change the world." Her voice dropped. "If there's one thing I learned from the story, it is this — Love isn't something you *think* about. It isn't something you *do*. It is *who you are*."

She paused as though searching for the right way to express what she felt. "If you are *thinking* about loving someone unconditionally, it is no longer unconditional love. It is very *conditional* love."

The young man let out his breath slowly. *Bravo!*

Robin twirled her hair. With a smile in her voice, she said, "And if you are *thinking* about being compassionate, usually what you're thinking is — *look at me, how compassionate I am!*"

Nervous laughter rippled through the room.

"And," interjected Jim, spreading his arms. "If you are *thinking* about being non-judgemental, *then it's too late*! The reason you were thinking about it is because you were judgemental in the first place!"

The whole room erupted.

Jim frowned. "How did this happen? How did we go so far afield?"

The young man sighed. "The problem is with our education system. And I'm not talking about just our schools and colleges. I'm also talking about how our experts and gurus teach us. And also, our corporate training programs."

Jim's eyes rounded.

The young man continued, "Over the years, our parents and our teachers and our gurus have been teaching us what to *do* and what to *think* and what to *say*."

He started pacing the length of the table. "And the only way to teach what to do and what to think is to teach us a whole slew of techniques and processes, rules and laws."

He exhaled slowly. "And when we focus on techniques and processes, love becomes a performance. Superficial. Unsatisfying. Completely ineffective."

He sat back down. "True love and true compassion come from within. They are a result of who we are, of how we see the world. And *that's* what they *should* be teaching us — how to shift our perspective, how to *see,* how to see *deeply* — so that love and compassion are an automatic and authentic *result* of how we see the world."

Tracy walked slowly to the table and laid her tea cup down. Everyone seemed to grasp the gravity of the moment and looked at her with anticipation. "I remember in the story, the Gardener wants to know what to do and what to say, but Father says — *Simply shift your perspective and everything else will follow.*"

She sat down as she continued quoting. "*It will be almost impossible to say anything ineffective. Almost everything you say will be effective.*"

She looked up. "We have become so conditioned to learning techniques and rules, we don't even realize how completely unnecessary they really are."

"Yes!" Robin nodded as her face lit up with recognition. "We don't even realize that they actually *get in the way*."

Todd swallowed. "Now I understand. In the story. What Father models is the *complete absence* of technique."

The young man smiled. "The best technique is *no* technique. The best rule is *no* rule. The best law is *no* law. The best process is *no* process."

Brian cupped his head in his hands. "I can't believe they've been teaching us everything backwards all these years."

Jim interrupted. "Are you saying we shouldn't be learning techniques? Don't we *need* people skills ... tricks for selling ... rules for leadership ... laws for success?"

The young man looked at Jim intently, his eyes creased with kindness. "The problem is most people use them as a crutch. As a substitute for shifting perspective."

Sandy pointed a finger to her forehead in a mock gesture. "Now I see why salespeople get such a bad rap. They've all been schooled in techniques. But no one wants to be technique*d*. What we all want is to be *seen*."

Brian was silent for a moment, his eyes far away. "On the flip side," he said softly, "I'd bet Father, who was the absence of technique, could have sold anything to anyone."

The young man felt a lump building in his throat.

Robin covered her mouth with her hand. "All these years, I've struggled with my rebellious teenager." Her eyes misted. "I've done everything *by the book*. But now I realize he doesn't need a *skilled* parent. What he needs is a parent who *sees* him."

Brian's lips quivered. "I had that problem with my relationship. I learned techniques for speaking with compassion, rules for active listening, processes for inquiring about what makes your partner happy."

He grimaced. "Now I see how superficial that all was. We were so blinded by process, we didn't really *see* each other." With a faraway look, he added, "We split up."

After a moment's reflection, Todd grunted. "At my company, they put us through lengthy leadership training. Taught us how to speak to inspire, run effective meetings, give praise, give feedback. I've walked on coals, climbed ropes, fallen back trustingly into others' arms. But despite all that training, I was never able to get that fierce loyalty from my team, that sense that each member is fully engaged." He smiled. "All the rules and laws in the world won't make you a great leader if you don't *see* your employees. Why didn't they teach me how to see?"

Sandy nodded. "No wonder everyone is complaining that there's never been a greater shortage of great leaders."

Jim chuckled. "Speaking of shortages, anyone notice the shortage of great customer service?"

Groans echoed through the room.

Sandy raised her eyebrows. "It's the same problem. They're taught everything but what they *need* to be taught. Lots of lines and scripts. Lots of reminders to change their attitudes, to put on a smile. But nothing about how to *see* people. If they don't know how to see people, they will never truly care. And if they don't care, how will they ever truly satisfy or delight their customers?"

Tracy clasped her hands together. "At our company, we've spent a lot of time and money on diversity training. We put everyone on a regimen of sensitivity classes. We've taught them how to embrace each others' differences. But the only thing that has really changed is discrimination and separation have gone underground."

The young man looked at Tracy. "Diversity, like love and compassion, is a *result* of how you see the world. You can't teach love. You can't teach compassion. In the same way, you can't teach diversity. All you can do is teach how to see the world. Then, and only then, will discrimination effortlessly become a *non-issue*."

The young man stood up. "Imagine a world in which we were all taught to change how we see the world."

"We would have great leaders," Todd volunteered.

"And great teamwork," added Tracy.

"And great customer service," Sandy said with a smile.

"Diversity would be a non-issue," Tracy offered.

"All our relationships would be deeper and more meaningful," Brian added.

"Great parents," Robin said, making a check-off sign with her forefinger.

Jim sat up. "The whole world would be different."

The young man closed his eyes, his hands crossed in front of him. "We will change the world."

Jim let out a slow whistle. "This is huge. Much bigger than I'd originally expected. It encompasses almost the entire spectrum of the human experience."

The young man nodded silently. He reflected back to the turning point in his life exactly seven months ago. Almost in a whisper, he said, "I'm beginning to realize that."

Have I understood it all?

He looked at Jim with kindly eyes. "It's been a remarkable journey of learning for me."

He elaborated, "They say the best way to learn anything — to really assimilate it, to *become* it — is to teach it to others. So, over the last few months, I've been facilitating small gatherings just like this. It turned out to be the best decision I made in my entire life."

He paused, then added, "With each group, I've learned so much. Each group has brought up points I'd never considered before. They've brought up questions that have required me to dig deeper and sharpen my perspective."

He rested his eyes on each individual. Robin. Brian. Sandy. Jim. Tracy. Todd. "And the best part is I've been making wonderful friends just like each of you here today."

The young man lowered his eyes. "There was one thing I learned that really surprised me."

The room filled with an expectant silence. He looked up. "I learned that you can't wait until the heat of the moment, when things are going awry, to shift your perspective. At that point, it is too late. You've already reacted. The other person has also reacted. After that, there's not much you can do or say, no magic technique you can pull from a hat to stop things from spiralling out of control."

He looked up. "Your only choice is to shift your perspective *now*, to lay the foundation *now*, before you ever need it."

Robin scratched her forehead. "I see what you mean."

The young man smiled. "This is about *becoming* the change as *a way of life*. It is about who you are in *every* moment."

He looked at Robin, then added, "Changing how I see the world has changed my day-to-day interactions, both personal and professional. I've been finding myself growing as a person. I've been surprised to find that I'm no longer unpredictable in my response when I encounter difficult people. I don't get angry. I don't get defensive. I don't get frustrated. I no longer say things I regret later. Instead, I remain unruffled without even thinking about it. I find myself moving through all types of situations with remarkable ease. The experience is something that words simply can't describe."

Robin raised her chin. "How can a lost person like me attain what you describe?"

The young man said, "Practice, practice, *practice* the change until you *become* it." He got up and turned to write on the blackboard. "Here is a great *free* resource:

Yes You Can Change The World.com

He looked around the room. "This a fun web site. Go visit it and set up a daily regimen of practice for yourself. Each day, practice sending a ripple to someone you know with the goal of surprising them that you see them in a way they never expected. The more you practice on this site, the better you will become at *automatically* shifting your perspective in your face-to-face interactions."

Jim leaned forward. "You know what? I was probably the most skeptical of the bunch when we first started this discussion. But now, I can't wait to get going. I want to practice the change and I want to spread the change."

He smiled at the young man. "I want to do what you are

doing today. How do I get started?"

The young man beamed. "Nothing would delight me more. It will be my privilege." He turned to the blackboard again. "Let me tell you about another great *free* resource:

SpreadChange.com

"At this site, you can get all kinds of help — talking points, discussion questions, promotional material, samples from others — to set up a group just like our group.

"The best part is if you are interested in reaching a certain type of group, you can get the materials specifically tailored to that group. You can choose materials for groups on leadership to relationships to parenting to spiritual — and everything in between. And if a group you're seeking is not available, you can request to set up a group where you collaborate with others all over the world to create the materials for the use of everyone involved."

Tracy's eyes beamed. "We're standing at the cusp of a revolution. A whole new era for humanity."

Todd nodded vigorously. "Did you know that every significant breakthrough in the world has been the result of us collectively breaking away from our old worldview?"

Tracy took his hand in hers. "And this is a whole new worldview of how to change the world."

Jim joined hands with Todd. "If we want to see a change

in the world, we must first change how we see the world."

Sandy took Jim's other hand. "We can make this change happen in our lifetime"

Brian held Sandy's other hand. "This is our legacy."

Robin reached for Brian's hand. "This is who we are."

The young man stepped into the circle and completed the chain by holding Todd's and Robin's free hands. "This *is* our legacy," he agreed.

He closed his eyes. "We all come into this world with nothing. We all leave this world with nothing. When we leave, all our symbols of success, all our possessions, all our acquisitions eventually become old, deteriorated, depleted or forgotten. The only things that stay alive, long after we're gone, are the relationships we create, the connections we make. The only things that remain eternal are the memories we forged with everyone we encountered. Our legacy is not our accomplishments or our possessions. It is the *quality* of our relationships.

"Sooner or later, we all have to ask ourselves — *Did I create fond memories or bitter memories?*

"We all have to ask ourselves — *In every encounter, in every interaction, in every connection, did I make the world better or worse?*

"We all have to ask ourselves — *What kind of person am I if I do not help make this world better?*"